BLUEPRINT FOR
LEARNING

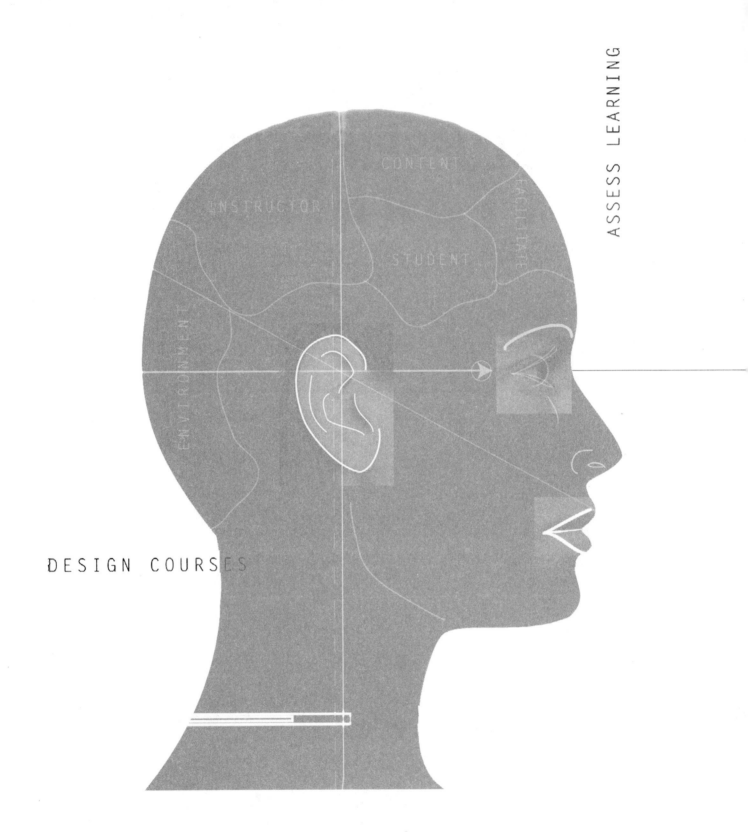

ASSESS LEARNING

CONTENT

INSTRUCTOR

STUDENT

ENVIRONMENT

DESIGN COURSES

BLUEPRINT FOR LEARNING

Constructing College Courses to Facilitate, Assess, and Document Learning

LAURIE RICHLIN

STERLING, VIRGINIA

Published by Stylus Publishing, LLC
22883 Quicksilver Drive
Sterling, Virginia 20166-2102

Book design and composition by Susan Mark
Coghill Composition Company
Richmond, Virginia

Library of Congress Cataloging-in-Publication-Data

Richlin, Laurie.
  Blueprint for learning : constructing college courses to facilitate, assess, and document
learning / Laurie Richlin.—1st ed.
      p.   cm.
    Includes bibliographical references and index.
    ISBN 1-57922-142-4 (cloth : alk. paper)—ISBN 1-57922-143-2 (pbk. : alk. paper)
    1. Education, Higher—Curricula.   2. Curriculum planning.   3. Curriculum
evaluation. 4. Educational accountability.   I. Title.
  LB2361.R476   2006
  378.1'99—dc22
                                           2005037174

ISBN: 1-57922-142-4 (cloth) / 13-digit ISBN: 978-1-57922-142-3
ISBN: 1-57922-143-2 (paper) / 13-digit ISBN: 978-1-57922-143-0

Printed in the United States of America

All first editions printed on acid-free paper that meets the American
National Standards Institute Z39-48 Standard.

Bulk Purchases
Quantity discounts are available for use
in workshops and for staff development.
Call 1-800-232-0223

First Edition, 2006

10 9 8 7 6 5 4 3 2

In appreciation of
Brenda Manning, for insisting on learning objectives

In memory of
Tony Grasha, *sine qua parum*

Contents

SECTION ONE
Course (Re)design

SECTION TWO
Facilitating Learning

SECTION THREE
Assessing Learning

SECTION FOUR
Documenting Learning

SECTION FIVE
Learning Resources and Planning Instruments

Preface

THIS BOOK IS BASED ON THE CURRENT DESIGN of a course that I have taught during the past 15 years (and continue to teach). The course has been redesigned each time I have taught it to incorporate what I learned from my students (in the course) and my faculty development colleagues (through their presentations and publications). The big question in college and university "teaching" is: How do we affect and effect maximum learning by our students? My hope in writing this book is that it will provide a blueprint for readers to select, design, and create learning experiences that will enable their own students to learn. My teaching goals (TGs) for this book are to enable readers to use concepts essential for promoting learning in designing a course in their discipline; to assess their effectiveness; and to document their course design in a portfolio and, perhaps, produce the Scholarship of Teaching and Learning (SoTL). The course itself has learning objectives (LOs) that include enabling participants to describe college/university course design elements; aspects of themselves, their students, the environment, and the course content that impact how their course is designed; effective practices for assessing student learning; and why they made their course design choices. My primary teaching objective of the course and this book is to create a full course design portfolio including the syllabus, questions to encourage discussion, assignments with rubrics, tests with blueprints, Classroom Assessment Techniques (CATs), and other teaching materials.

Having been trained as a scholar of higher education, when I began my work as a faculty development professional, I brought with me the important concept of "fit." In order for faculty members to teach successfully, I think it is necessary for them to understand the differences among individual colleges and universities in terms of who their colleagues and students are, the culture of their departments, and the institutional expecta-

tions for their time. All of these elements are important both for course design and for faculty job satisfaction.

I have found during my work with faculty members at both small and large colleges and universities that, although professors have deep concern for their students' learning, most have no way of grasping the complex problems of teaching and learning. Nor should they know how to improve learning: In almost all cases no one has ever taught them anything about the subject. Just as we would not expect our students to acquire the ability to perform complex tasks without study, practice, and feedback, we should not expect college instructors to learn to teach effectively without similar processes.

During the years I have developed the concepts and processes in this book, there have been several important changes in what we know about the teaching><learning (T><L) connection. The T><L connection is the interplay between aspects of an instructor's teaching activities and the learning needs of students. A good T><L connection provides active experiences and feedback so that students have many opportunities to hear about or observe new material, try it out, and work toward mastery.

The most important change is the move from efforts to improve teaching to those that improve learning. Indeed, it is learning that now is center stage in higher education. Barr and Tagg (1995) call this a change from the "instruction paradigm" to a "learning paradigm." Although all of the changes they discuss impact course design, the ones about the nature of learning are of particular importance. In Barr and Tagg's chart "Comparing Educational Paradigms" (p. 16), the *Instruction Paradigm* defines learning as something an instructor feeds in doses to passive students; in the *Learning Paradigm,* students "must be active discoverers and constructors of their own knowledge." The Learning Paradigm changes the "Mission and Purpose" of colleges and universities from "offering courses and programs" to "creating powerful learning environments," from "providing/delivering instruction" to "producing learning." In addition, it changes the role of instructors from "disciplinary experts who impart knowledge by lecturing" to designers of learning environments. That is what this book is about.

Teaching is a messy business, so this book will not enable you to design a *perfect* course, because there is no such thing. Each time you teach a course you are at a different point in your life, you have another group of students, the place and time you teach are different, and the course content has advanced. Every once in a while all of the elements will come together: you are at your best, your students are actively involved, you have an environment conducive to implementing the best kinds

of experiences for students to learn the material, and the content seems particularly captivating to all. Enjoy that experience; it is magical, but not predictable. What interacting with this book *will* enable you to do is to utilize the best practices to continue to redesign your courses to better meet your teaching goals and the learning needs of your students. It will provide a blueprint, a scholarly scaffold, and a documentation strategy for your efforts and accomplishments.

Scholarly design is an ongoing process that begins with a full understanding of how students learn and what experiences best facilitate their learning in each discipline. It concludes with an assessment of how well students have learned and a public reassessment of the course design. This book will guide you through those design and documentation steps.

Acknowledgments

I OWE A DEBT OF GRATITUDE, OF COURSE, TO THE many people who assisted me in developing this process and writing this book.

Brenda Manning, to whom this book is dedicated, taught me about learning objectives, insisted on learning objectives, and then insisted again. She also was the generous coauthor of our 1995 book, *Improving a College/University Teaching Evaluation System,* on evaluating teaching through course portfolios.

Tony Grasha left us with a gold mine of ideas, concepts, research data, and optimism for becoming better teachers. His thoughts continue to support and inspire us. Without him we would have had so much less.

I have been a fan of Tom Angelo and Pat Cross's work with teaching goals and Classroom Assessment Techniques (CATs) since I knew they existed. CATs remain the best way I have found to help instructors develop into learning-centered teachers.

My faculty development colleagues, especially those involved with graduate student preparation, have provided me with research-based, innovative ideas that have contributed to my understanding of the teaching><learning process. Shirley Ronkowski, Laura Border, Julie-Ann McFann, and Nancy Chism—as well as other Professional and Organizational Development (POD) Network in Higher Education colleagues—have, in particular, led the way.

As she has done for most of my professional career, my daughter, Jennifer Stokely, provided structural and copy editing for my work, untangling my thoughts and syntax and cleaning up my grammar.

During the time I have developed the course design process, Milt Cox has brought to it valuable new ideas from his own work in mathematics and faculty development. In addition, as the founder and director of a quarter-century of the Lilly Conference on College Teaching, and as the founder and editor-in-chief of the *Journal on Excellence in College Teaching,* he has provided both in-person and published forums for the best thinkers on college teaching to share their Scholarship of Teaching and Learning among themselves and with others. I also have learned a great deal from the participants and authors who have contributed their work to the conferences and the journal.

Hundreds of faculty members who have attended my course design workshops and students in my teaching assistant development and preparing future faculty courses have worked through the portfolio design process, and their feedback has improved it greatly. In particular, I thank the 2004–2005 Claremont Graduate University Preparing Future Faculty Fellows who read and reread drafts of the manuscript, edited each draft, and tried out the processes and products as written, all the while remaining cheerful and supportive: John Alexander, psychology; Erin Andrade-Lopez, education; Al Arboleda, information science; Marlene Biseda, executive management; Ariana Brooks, psychology; LaMesha Carter, education; Nathan Garrett, information science; Akiko Otsu, education; Robin Owens, religion; Edward Robinson, cultural studies; Elizabeth Seward, education; Kelly Thompson Eggertsen, English; Moana Vercoe, politics and economics; Dorothea Kahena Viale, women's studies in religion; and, especially, Paul Witman, information science.

I am grateful to the American Psychological Association for granting permission to use the materials in Resource 2: Learner-Centered Psychological Principles, on pages 115–118; and to Allyn and Bacon for granting permission to use material from *A Taxonomy for Learning, Teaching, and Assessing* (2001), by Lorin W. Anderson and David R. Krathwohl, in the table on page 123.

John von Knorring, president and publisher of Stylus Publishing, LLC, and Stylus editors provided feedback, creative suggestions, and large amounts of patience to bring this project to completion.

Thank you all.

Introduction

SHIRLEY RONKOWSKI

*The scientist [scholar] is not a person who gives the right answers,
he [she] is one who asks the right questions.*

CLAUDE LEVI-STRAUSS

DURING THE TWENTY-FIVE YEARS IN WHICH I'VE BEEN involved in university level instructional development, I have taught hundreds of courses and seminars on the topics discussed in *Blueprint for Learning*. What I find so useful about this book is that it brings together the academic research of the past quarter century, models its use, and then challenges readers to do the same. The book identifies the processes that scholarly teachers use in their teaching and in communicating new knowledge about instruction to their colleagues. The author models a scholarly approach, engaging the research findings on teaching and learning in higher education to form new perspectives, approaches, and rubrics for their practical application.

The body of research reported here is done in ways that encourage us to ask the "right questions" to improve student learning in our courses. It is likely that you will find yourself interacting with the content of these pages by questioning your own instructional design and creating new ideas for your courses as you read. No doubt you will note some of the practical ideas given as ones you currently use and others as ones that give you a slightly new slant on old ideas. If you are not already familiar with the literature on teaching and learning, much of the theoretical content will be completely new to you. For those who are already familiar with this material, *Blueprint* cogently summarizes the major research and provides some twists and turns along the way that provide a new look at familiar territory.

The author follows her own "blueprint" by beginning each chapter with a statement of the intended learning objectives, which are at the cognitive taxonomy levels of *remember* and *understand* in the early chapters and advance into critical thinking levels of *analysis, evaluation,* and *creation* in later chapters. Many of us will conclude our reading of each chapter by questioning the extent to which we are able to fulfill the stated goals. More importantly, the book presents research literature in ways that make it difficult for us *not* to question our own course designs. The chapter on teaching and learning styles will prompt questions as to how these styles interact to affect the teaching and learning in our courses. Practical application of the current versions of the Bloom taxonomies of cognitive, affective, and psychomotor skills guides us to ask whether or not our assessment tools are congruent with our stated learning objectives and chosen learning activities. John Andrew's Question Typography in chapter 16 gives us pause as we ask ourselves what types of questions we need to be asking to increase student response rate.

The final section provides the reader with resources to reflect upon teaching styles, learning styles, motivation, individual differences, and much more, and then to put the results of those reflections into action. Numerous rubrics give us templates to help respond to some of the questions that undoubtedly have arisen about how our own students are learning as we read through the earlier chapters. These rubrics can be used as templates for activities such as writing learning objectives, implementing learning activities, and assessing student learning.

In addition to assisting individual faculty members in their professional growth, *Blueprint* will be useful in many different situations: as a framework for organizing the content of orientation programs and multiple-day workshops for new and future faculty; as a guide for programs that assist faculty in their own professional development; and by faculty learning communities to deepen their understanding and practice of the teaching>\<learning™ connection. It will make an excellent guide for programs that seek to assist faculty in their own professional development, and faculty learning communities will find it helpful in deepening their understanding and practice of the teaching>\<learning connection.

Shirley Ronkowski, Ph.D, *has been a teaching consultant and the director of the campus-wide Teaching Assistant Development Program at the University of California, Santa Barbara since 1983. A former faculty member of the School of Education at California Lutheran University, she has contributed dozens of presentations and pre-conference workshops for organizations such as AERA, AAHE, POD, AACE, SITE, and TechEd. Dr. Ronkowski has consulted on professional development and the adoption of instructional technology at numerous community colleges, and was the instructional designer for a FIPSE grant at Santa Barbara City College to develop online learning and pedagogical materials <www.studenthub.org> and <www.studenthub.org/faculty>. Her published articles, book chapters, and conference papers focus on instructional design, the scholarship of teaching, cooperative learning, and instructional technology for both current and future faculty.*

SECTION ONE

Course (Re)Design

THIS SECTION DESCRIBES A PROCESS FOR CREATING, IMPLEMENTING, AS-sessing, documenting, and (re)designing successful learning connections with your students. To design a course that facilitates learning, you will begin by considering aspects of yourself and of your students, the environment of the course you will be teaching, and a multitude of elements in the content you select for that course. With that information, you will be able to identify course teaching goals; review the results of what others have done; and design student learning objectives, learning activities, and assessment procedures. By analyzing your results, you will be able to incorporate what you have learned into your redesign for the next time you teach the course. If your results are worth sharing, you will place them in the context of teaching and learning in higher education and submit your manuscript for peer review. If accepted, you will disseminate your work through presentation and publication, placing it into the knowledge base of teaching and learning.

CHAPTER 1

Scholarly Teaching and the Scholarship of Teaching and Learning

LEARNING OBJECTIVES

Readers of this chapter will be able to:

- Define Scholarly Teaching and the Scholarship of Teaching and Learning.
- Describe the differences between them.
- Describe the steps in the scholarly process.

WHETHER YOU ARE A SCHOLAR OF MEDIEVAL HIStory or physics, you follow scholarly processes that are specific to your discipline. The scholarly process of teaching uses a social science approach similar to the process you used in doing research reports in college: Define your needs (in this case, helping students reach learning objectives), consult the literature, choose and implement methods, document findings, analyze results, obtain feedback, and adapt teaching methods and learning experiences accordingly for the next time you teach that course.

Since 1990, faculty, administrators and faculty development professionals have been working to understand and implement what the Carnegie Foundation described as the four appropriate types of scholarship for the American faculty: the scholarships of Discovery, Integration, Application/Practice, and Teaching (Boyer, 1990). Unfortunately, the concept of a scholarship of teaching became mixed up with the act of teaching itself. Actually, two different activities are involved: scholarly teaching and the resulting scholarship (Richlin, 1993, 1998). Scholarly teaching and the Scholarship of Teaching and Learning (SoTL) are closely interrelated, but they differ in both their intent and product. Because both are vital to the life of the academy, it is necessary to clarify

and operationalize each of them (Richlin, 1993, 2001).

Scholarly teaching (Figure 1.1) is a method of designing and implementing a course to improve the learning of the students in the course. A scholarly instructor collects materials and reflects on observations throughout the course, systematically documenting them. The best

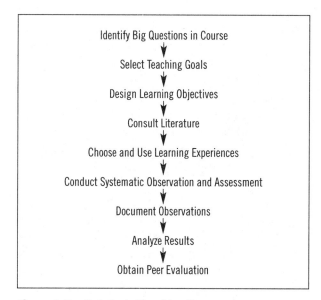

Figure 1.1   Scholarly Teaching Process

format for documenting observations is a course design portfolio. By concentrating on achieving student learning objectives in an individual course, you can update your design each time you teach, based on what your students learned in the previous course. Section 4 provides scaffolding for creating a course design portfolio.

After the course is over, you are able to analyze the information you collected during the course. What types of questions did the students miss on tests? What parts of assignments confused the students? Was the level of the objectives, work, and grading appropriate for your students? Did you have the necessary resources? What adaptations will you make the next time you teach?

Submitting work for peer review is part of all scholarly processes. Teaching or course portfolios may be submitted to one's department, a special campus committee, or peers at other institutions. The assessment of the course is focused on materials and student work and also may include observations of class sessions. This evaluation of teaching is more authentic than evaluations based on inputs such as counting the instructor's use of examples or asking students to compare the course with other courses. Using the course portfolio enables you to compare your results to what you had observed before you began, in order to determine how well the teaching experiences you chose resulted in student learning.

The *Scholarship of Teaching and Learning*, or SoTL (Figure 1.2), on the other hand, is a formal, peer-reviewed communication in an appropriate media and venue that becomes part of the knowledge base of teaching and learning in higher education. Once you have created course learning objectives, the most useful activity is to find out what others have done to meet similar objectives. Consulting the literature these days includes not only reading peer-reviewed articles and books, but also searching the Web, attending disciplinary and multidisciplinary conference sessions on teaching, and participating in faculty learning communities and on listservs with other instructors.

College instructors usually make their teaching decisions implicitly—and oftentimes in the midst of a live classroom situation. Although I believe that most professors make good professional decisions on course activities, methods, and assessment, if those decisions are not clarified, they cannot be evaluated and improved. As executive editor of the *Journal on Excellence in College Teaching*, the major multidisciplinary, peer-

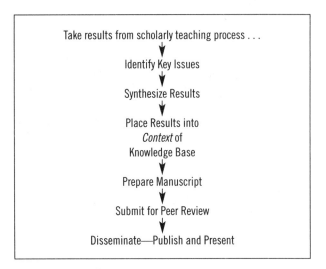

Figure 1.2   Scholarship of Teaching and Learning

reviewed journal on college teaching and learning, I read hundreds of manuscripts each year. Most have to be returned to the authors without being sent for external review because they report only "this is what we did, and everybody loved it." They often describe in great detail what they did and often supply feedback from students on how much better they *think* they learned, but this does not constitute data or research. My "standard" letter of rejection reads as follows:

> Thank you for submitting your manuscript. Unfortunately, we are unable to publish it. In order to be of use to our readers, you would need to explain *why* you did what you did. What did you *see* in your students' behavior (test scores, class participation, writing) that led you to believe you needed to change your current methods in order for them to better meet the learning objectives? Why did you choose this method to meet your goals and their objectives? What have others done in a similar situation? What learning objectives results were you trying to improve? What evidence do you have on how your students were meeting those objectives *before* you implemented your changes so you can compare that evidence with your current results?

Naturally, the authors cannot answer those questions if they have not designed their course in a scholarly way. As Richard Light and colleagues say, "*You cannot save by analysis what you bungle by design*" (Light, Wilett, & Singer, 1990, p. viii, italics in original).

Finding out what others have done, whether in your discipline or another, can save you from repeating mistakes. You can share what you have learned from your students and receive additional feedback through participation in both disciplinary and multidisciplinary conferences on teaching and learning. Associations such as the American Mathematical Society, American Psychological Association, and American Sociological Association hold annual conferences with presentation tracks for teaching, as well as separate, focused teaching conferences.

The Lilly Conferences on College and University Teaching, held in five regions of the United States, have been providing an interdisciplinary forum for the Scholarship of Teaching and Learning since 1980. More than 650 participants attend the original conference in Oxford, Ohio, each year, and about 200 people attend each of the regional ones. The Lilly Conferences encourage faculty members to bring their results to the conference to receive feedback from colleagues before submitting a manuscript for publication. It is when you make your work public, through presentation and publication, that it enters the knowledge base and becomes scholarship. Your work will inform others as they make their teaching decisions.

CHAPTER 2

Scholarly Design Process

LEARNING OBJECTIVES

Readers of this chapter will be able to:

- Describe each of the steps in the design cycle.
- Describe the four elements to consider when designing a specific course.

THE BLUEPRINT OF THE SCHOLARLY CYCLE OF COURSE (Re)Design in Figure 2.1 involves multiple levels of elements and activities that form a continual design/redesign process. In only a few cases do courses play out exactly as they are planned. As we teach, we see areas where we should cut and others where we should expand. By following the scholarly design cycle we can continue to improve student learning each time we teach the course. For each specific course you are planning, the four elements that interact to form the basis for your teaching goals and student learning objectives are you, your students, the environment, and the content. Both you and the students bring to the learning experience a variety of characteristics, such as learning styles, interests, expertise, and personal history. A course is scheduled in a particular room at a specific time, day, and season. As everyone who has been a college student knows, learning is different at 8:00 A.M. than at 8:00 P.M., on Monday morning or Friday afternoon than on other days, and during a blizzard than on an 80-degree spring day. The content, even for introductory courses, changes over time. New texts and resources, especially technology, become available; new departmental or campuswide initiatives add course requirements.

Teaching *hopes* translate the big questions of your discipline into what you want for your students. Hopes do not need to be teachable or assessable. They can include affective terms such as *appreciate*. Hopes are long term. For instance, one professor in a recent workshop hoped her students would learn to "love medieval literature," even though it would be difficult (and perhaps unethical) to teach and evaluate love.

In a 15-year study, Ken Bain and colleagues identified and interviewed almost a hundred extraordinary college teachers in a wide range of disciplines and institutions. These teachers were considered good teachers because they "achieved remarkable success in helping their students learn in ways that made a sustained, substantial, and positive influence on how these students think, act, and feel" (Bain, 2004, p. 5). This study states, "The best teachers ask themselves what they hope students can do intellectually, physically, or emotionally by the end of the course and why those abilities are important" (p. 95). You can have any types of hopes you want for your course. *Teaching goals* (TGs) represent *your* intentions for the course. Meeting the teaching goals will be *your* accomplishment as an instructor. Choosing your goals involves considering elements about you, your students, the environment, and the content. This is where those elements combine to focus on selecting the content for

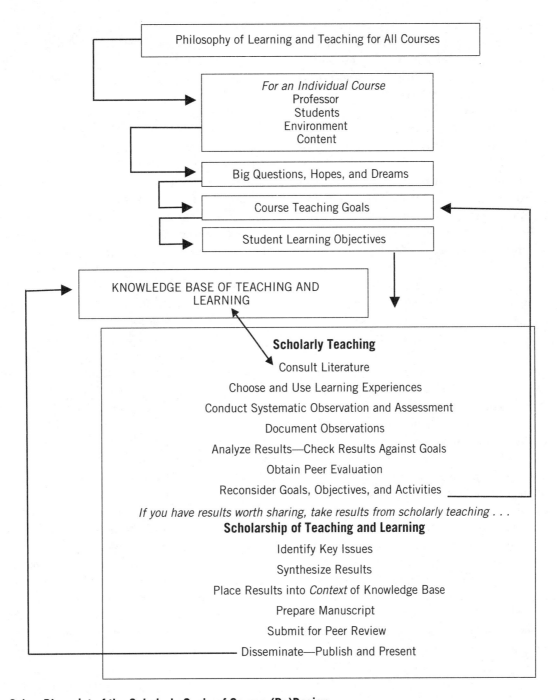

Figure 2.1.   Blueprint of the Scholarly Cycle of Course (Re)Design

the course. Goals translate your hopes into more specific plans.

Student *learning objectives* (LOs) are where the "rubber meets the road." Changing teaching goals into student learning objectives is *the most important step* in designing a course. One of the ways that the professors in the Bain (2004) study were identified as outstanding

teachers was that "colleagues in [their] field or in a closely related field would regard [their] learning objectives as worthy and substantial" (p. 8). The professors in the Bain study "engage in an extensive examination of their learning objectives, reviewing students' work as a reflection of the learning, analyzing the kinds of standards and methods used in assessing that work, and looking closely at the levels of learning expected. To assess their learning objectives, they follow important intellectual developments emerging within and outside their disciplines" (p. 164). LOs belong to students because they are the ones who will achieve them. Because we cannot "see" learning otherwise, learning objectives must be observable and measurable; they need to state exactly what the student will be able to *do* after participating in a course.

An amazing result of Bain's (2004) study of exceptional teachers is that the "best teaching can not be found in particular practices or rules but in the *attitudes* of the teachers, in their *faith* in their students' abilities to achieve, in their *willingness* to take their students seriously and to let them assume control of their own education, and in their *commitment* to let all policies and practices flow from central learning objectives and from a mutual respect and agreement between students and teachers" (pp. 78–79). According to Bain,

> The professors do in class what they think will best help and encourage their students to learn outside of class, between one meeting and the next. . . . The difference comes in the planning and in why teachers make their choices. Because the best teachers plan their courses backward, deciding what students should be able to do by the end of the semester, they map a series of intellectual developments through the course, with the goal of encouraging students to learn on their own, engaging them in deep thinking. In ordinary classes, instructors might create assignments for students, but they rarely use the class to help students do the work. (p. 114)

Designing learning activities involves an understanding of how your students learn and of the range of your available teaching behaviors. In section 2, you will work with student learning styles and cognitive development. It is the match between your students' learning styles and your preferred teaching styles that creates a vital teaching>>learning connection. You have strengths and preferences for how you teach. The activities connected to your teaching style will reach different types of learners. As you match learning experiences to learning objectives you also will consider your own range of behavior. Are you an exciting lecturer? Have you developed connections in the community that can provide internships? Do you enjoy climbing up on the desk dressed as Shakespeare declaiming verse? Or do you prefer to facilitate role-playing scenarios? Whatever the learning objectives, the activities have to combine how your students learn best with what you do best. Chapter 16 provides a wide range of possible learning experiences for you to adapt for your own courses.

Part of what you will design for your course is an assessment process based on the learning objectives you have selected. Assessment includes student products, such as tests and papers, as well as feedback from colleagues and students. By building into your course the ways you plan to evaluate how well your students achieve their learning objectives, you will have information about how to improve the course in the future. We will work with assessment in section 3.

The next parts of the process are documenting your observations of students' progress in the course, analyzing the learning results, and obtaining peer evaluation of your course through a teaching or course portfolio. After you check the results against your goals and objectives, you can determine how to proceed. You can reconsider your goals, objectives, and learning activities and reenter the design process. If you have results worth sharing, you can enter the process of the Scholarship of Teaching and Learning.

CHAPTER 3

Professor

LEARNING OBJECTIVES

Readers of this chapter will be able to:

- Describe characteristics of instructors that affect course design.
- Describe how instructors' view of difference can affect learning.

THE FIRST CONSIDERATION IN DESIGN IS THE MOST important element: *you*, the instructor. Who you are, what you believe, and what you know set the boundaries of your course.

Consider who you are as a person and as a teacher. Where did you go to college and graduate school? Was it in a similar or different type of institution than the one in which you are teaching? Do you have young children or elderly parents? Consider how you spend your time: Are you writing an article (or a dissertation)? doing research? teaching three or more courses? driving the carpool to soccer?

Your other obligations, including other courses you are teaching, can limit the time you have to devote to *this* course and will, therefore, have an impact on what learning experiences (LEs) you can use. With limited time, you may not be able to grade essays promptly, which works against the principle of prompt feedback for learning. On the other hand, if you have a large amount of time to devote to the course, you will be able to provide prompt feedback on essays, arrange and participate with your students in service-learning activities, and be able to try out new learning activities that will require time to implement.

All of the elements that make you who you are go into how you design and conduct your courses. The Bain (2004) study showed that an instructor's attitudes toward students and difference have a large impact on how well students learn. The exceptional teachers saw themselves as "fellow students—no, fellow human beings—struggling with the mysteries of the universe, human society, historical development, or whatever. . . . A sense of awe at the world and the human condition stood at the center of their relationships with their students" (p. 144).

How people feel about difference also plays into their course designs. Margaret Matlin (1991), winner of the American Psychological Association's Teaching of Psychology award and author of several psychology textbooks, relates the "social cognition approach to stereotypes" to teaching. *Subject* variables, she explains, are the actual characteristics of individual people, such as age, political view, work experience, and learning style. It is important to determine and understand students' subject variables to aid in their learning.

On the other hand, *stimulus* variables are in the perception of the onlooker, such as the instructor or other students, and come from family attitudes, experience with people different from ourselves, and education. Matlin (1991) gives this example:

> [I]f we are interested in studying gender as a stimulus variable, we ask people to make judgments about males versus females. We want to know whether people in general have different thoughts about males than they have about females. For instance, we might ask people to guess how well a college freshman named John would do on a mathematics test, compared with a college freshman named Jane. Chances are people would predict John would do substantially better. Therefore, gender as a stimulus variable is typically fairly important. In fact, gender as a stimulus variable is generally more important than gender as a subject variable. . . . People tend to believe stereotypes about men and women that are not supported by reality. (p. 10)

Stimulus variables lead to stereotypes, which can deter learning. Stereotypes influence our teaching behavior in several ways. One is that "we are more likely to focus our attention on a particular behavior that is consistent with our expectations. . . . If an economics professor has a stereotype that females are not very knowledgeable about financial issues, the professor may notice an error in a female student's midterm essay, but may fail to pay attention to the next sentence, which contains a strong, insightful point" (Matlin, 1991, p. 14).

A second way that stereotyping can influence teaching is if the instructor categorizes people into groups and teaches to the stereotypes instead of to individual students. Matlin cites the following quote by Fiske and Taylor (1984) in her article "The Social Cognition Approach to Stereotypes and Its Application to Teaching": "The tendency to see outgroup members as highly similar to one another has an interesting effect: People make rash predictions about a whole group of outsiders on the basis of meeting only one of them" (Matlin, 1991, p. 15).

A third way that stereotyping can influence teaching is by the perception of what a person does. Matlin (1991) uses this example: "A college student who is sarcastic may be perceived as spiteful if the student is female, but cynical if the student is male" (p. 16).

One of the professors in the Bain (2004) study wrote the following:

> Our ideas about who belongs in school are too often rooted in prejudices about class and place and even language—let alone about race or ethnicity. When I make judgments about students' suitability for the next level of study in my field—as I do every time I assign a grade or counsel a student about her career—I have to make sure I have derived whatever puny stab I can make at a good decision from good data and good reasoning. Thus, I must worry about the kind of examinations I give, how I interpret the results of those tests, and what else I might use to "grade" a student. (pp. 77–78)

How do you like to approach new tasks? Do you prefer to reflect first and act later or to jump right into the task? Consider how your preferences influence your teaching and their impact on your students' learning. How do you like to learn? In what types of learning experiences would you like to participate with your students in this course? Do you want to work with the community? Do you want to develop new artistic techniques? Do you enjoy the give-and-take of classroom discussions? Consider how your preferences might compare with those of your students.

You also have your own styles of learning and teaching. As you will see in section 2, what is important is the match between your preferred teaching styles and your students' learning styles. Learners learn best from certain types of instruction. Most first-year students come to campus as dependent learners, expecting professors to be experts who provide information through lectures. As students mature, they require facilitation of their independent learning so that they can develop their critical-thinking skills. You will be more comfortable with some teaching behaviors than others and will stretch to provide some of the types of learning experiences that will help your students learn best.

Have you had professional experience in the "real world" in the field in which you teach? Your professional experience brings another strength into your course. If you have taught this course before, you will bring into the course design your memories—positive and negative—of how you and your students inter- acted. Another consideration is whether you have all of the necessary expertise to optimize student learning. Are there skills that you need to "import" through training, a coteacher or consultant, or technology? For instance, if there are learning experiences that you would like to be able to implement but that you do not feel ready to conduct, contact your department or campus faculty development office for support. The people there also may know other instructors who have experiences they can share with you. In addition, as described in chapter 5, you can assemble a faculty learning community of colleagues to study the meth- ods with you.

Students

LEARNING OBJECTIVES

Readers of this chapter will be able to:

- Describe characteristics of students that affect their learning.

BAIN (2004) REPORTS THAT "THE BEST TEACHERS TRY to find out as much as possible about their students' . . . ambitions, their approaches to and conceptions of learning, the ways they reasoned, the mental models they brought with them, their temperaments, their habits of heart and mind, and the daily matters that occupied their attention" (p. 157).

PERSONAL CHARACTERISTICS

Student demographics and life experiences play into course design. Nontraditional-age students bring skills and knowledge that we may not have, but that they can share with us and their classmates. For instance, students may be professionals in the same field as the course, have traveled extensively, or have relevant life experiences. Learning from students is one of the benefits of college and university teaching because it deepens your own knowledge. Not including their input limits students' full participation and denies you fresh insights.

COGNITIVE LEVEL

The developmental schemes described in section 2 will help you and your students to understand their cognitive development, motivations, and preferences so that you can design your course to meet them most efficiently. Some instructors have their students complete various inventories in order to help students understand how they learn and strategies for achievement.

LEARNING STYLES

Students have preferred styles of learning, some of which cross all fields and others that they favor in certain situations. Learning experiences can be tailored to your students' strengths while including strategies that will help them strengthen their learning weaknesses.

CHAPTER 5

Environment

LEARNING OBJECTIVES

Readers of this chapter will be able to:

- Describe three types of teaching and learning environments.
- Describe benefits and challenges of each type of learning environment.

ENVIRONMENTAL ELEMENTS IMPACT HOW A COURSE can be conducted and, therefore, how it should be designed. These elements can be divided into outside, classroom, and online.

OUTSIDE ENVIRONMENT

Outside elements include the type and traditions of the institution and discipline, departmental policies, and even the time of day or season that the course is scheduled. Different types of colleges and universities provide different opportunities for student learning. Small, residential, four-year institutions, for instance, provide a learning environment different from large, commuter universities. When students live on campus, they have more opportunities to meet with each other and to know each other outside the classroom. Commuters, on the other hand, spend a minimum of time on campus and usually find it difficult to find opportunities to meet other students in person.

Surrounding communities can provide a variety of resources to enhance classroom learning. What is available in your community that you can include in your learning activities? Consider possible volunteer activities, people with special expertise, and even natural wonders that can expand the opportunities for your students to learn.

The season, day, and time of day for which you are designing your course can make a considerable difference. You have your own best times of day for active work, as do your students. The same group of people act and interact differently at 8:00 A.M. than they do at 8:00 P.M. Usually, though, students who attend classes during the day are more traditional aged and those who attend evening classes are older students who have been at work all day. Almost everywhere the weather is more unpredictable during the winter and spring terms than during the fall, and in colder climates, the weather during late fall can pose problems, as well.

Institutional policies can have a big impact on your design. Does your institution or department require you to use a particular text or even a departmental syllabus? Is there a departmental final for all students in sections of the course you teach? Is there an attendance policy? Is there a policy on late work or missed tests? All of these policies need to be considered and, sometimes, worked around, as you design your course.

A supportive institutional teaching culture can provide additional resources for improving teaching and learning. Many terms are associated with the groups on campus and beyond who are dedicated to improving college and university teaching. Some of them are *faculty development, instructional development, professional development,* and *organizational development.* These functions usually are located in teaching centers or offices with names such as Faculty Development Center or Office of Teaching Excellence. Faculty development efforts range from individual consulting with faculty members about specific courses to workshops to longer-range efforts such as faculty learning communities (FLCs), discussed later.

Faculty members and faculty development professionals also have formed local, regional, and national associations to promote teaching excellence. In Canada, the Society for Teaching and Learning in Higher Education (STLHE), which produced the Ethical Principles in University Teaching discussed in chapter 15, is a group of faculty members, administrators, and faculty development professionals who meet annually and communicate through newsletters and on a listserv. STLHE also publishes a series of books on teaching. In the United States, the Professional and Organizational Development (POD) Network in Higher Education has more than 1,500 members, primarily U.S. faculty development professionals. POD has an annual conference, publishes both a newsletter and a peer-reviewed journal, and has a very active listserv. Similar organizations exist around the world and, including STLHE and POD, have formed the International Consortium of Educational Developers, which holds a conference biannually. The International Alliance of Teacher Scholars (IATS) was formed in 1989 to expand to other venues the Lilly Conference on College Teaching, which originated at Miami University in 1980. IATS has sponsored regional Lilly conferences in Southern California, New England, Maryland, Georgia, Texas, Michigan, Oregon, and the United Kingdom.

Over the past 20 years, most faculty development efforts have been onetime workshops, lasting from an hour to as long as two weeks, on various teaching topics and techniques. Unfortunately, this type of experience does not utilize the principles in the "Seven Principles for Good Practice in Undergraduate Education" (Chickering & Gamson, 1987), which are applicable to all teaching><learning experiences. Chickering and Gamson state that good practice encourages student-faculty contact, cooperation among students, and active learning; gives prompt feedback; emphasizes time on task; communicates high expectations; and respects diverse talents and ways of learning. A more detailed ex-

planation of the Seven Principles can be found in chapter 16. In traditional faculty development activities, faculty members spend time together at a workshop but are left by themselves to try out the new ideas they may have for designing new learning experiences (LEs) with no further "faculty-student" (workshop leader–faculty member) contact, no feedback, and none of the other Seven Principles.

College and university teachers, just like their students, have a higher chance of learning if the Seven Principles are employed. A very successful model for providing that support is the faculty learning community, developed over the past 25 years at Miami University. This model has spread to hundreds of colleges and universities through conferences, institutes, consulting, regional and national grants, and publications. FLCs are cross-disciplinary communities of 6–20 (8–12 recommended) faculty members and, sometimes, professional staff and graduate students. Participants are selected to create a diverse group in terms of field, experience, and other criteria particular to the various FLCs. Some FLCs are cohort based, such as those including only new, junior, or senior faculty members. Others are topic based with a curriculum addressing a particular issue or challenge in the classroom or on campus. Topics have ranged from assessment to information literacy to teaching women's studies courses.[1] In almost all FLCs, participants choose a focus course for a project to improve student learning.

The results on increasing student learning on a campus supporting FLC programs are very encouraging. Milton Cox, the originator of and advocate for FLCs, compares FLC outcomes with those of student learning communities (Cox, 2004). These include retention; deeper and more complex learning; personal, social, and professional development; sensitivity to and respect for other points of view; and higher civic contributions, such as participation in campus government. Figure 5.1 presents results from a survey of 50 past FLC participants. Faculty respondents reported that they were aware of increased student learning in their classrooms after participating in an FLC. The positive effects they perceived were more successful achievement of existing and new learning objectives, greater student interest,

---

[1]A full listing of 2003–2004 FLCs by institution, cohort type, and topic is available at http://www.cgu.edu/include/FLCList.xls. Extensive information on building FLCs can be found at http://www.units.muohio.edu/flc/.

Reported Change after Participating in FLC *"Increase in students' ability to . . ."*	Respondents Reporting the Change (%)	Change (on 4-point scale)
apply principles and generalizations already learned to new problems and solutions	94	3.0
ask good questions	94	3.0
develop an openness to new ideas	94	3.0
work productively with others	96	3.2
think for themselves	92	3.0
synthesize and integrate information and ideas	98	3.1

Figure 5.1   Perceived Impact of Faculty Learning Community Participation on Student Learning

Source: Based on a survey of 50 past participants in Miami University Faculty Learning Communities (Cox, 1994, pp. 11–12). The survey was adapted from the Angelo and Cross (1993) "Teaching Goal Inventory."

better classroom atmosphere, more positive student evaluation comments, and better papers or writing assignments. Faculty respondents also reported that—as a result of their participation in an FLC—their students' learning increased because they, the faculty members, had greater enthusiasm about teaching and learning (98%); understood scholarly teaching and the scholarship of teaching and learning (98%), and were more reflective (94%), confident (90%), and revitalized (90%) (Cox, 2004, p. 12).

FLCs meet an average of every two to three weeks, often over a meal, to discuss a particular topic of interest, often with a presentation by one of the members, and to discuss how the individual projects are progressing. In addition, FLC members participate in retreats and national conferences and may have a faculty or student partner. FLC meetings and activities periodically include family members and mentors. FLCs incorporate the seven principles with a few adaptations:

- Student-Faculty Contact is mirrored by Peer Contact.
- Cooperation Among Students becomes Cooperation Among Participants.
- Active Learning is incorporated into the meetings and other activities.
- Participants give Prompt Feedback for each other's projects.
- Time on Task is increased through focused, regular meetings.
- Each member provides High Expectations for the others.

- Diverse Talents and Ways of Learning are essential to the success of the FLC and are addressed when selecting the participants.

CLASSROOM ENVIRONMENT

Classroom environments range from the physical facility, number of students, and ambience to the presence or absence of additional instructors such as teaching assistants. We all are used to learning and teaching in a variety of room settings. Paul Cornell (2002) states

Until recently [learning environments] were built to enable a teacher to deliver a message to a large group, which sat in silence, dutifully listening and taking notes. Rooms were rectangular or wedge-shaped and the focus—and attention—was directed to the front where the instructor exercised complete control of the pace, content, and sequence of activities. Teaching varied little, so the furniture was optimized and bolted into place. (p. 33)

He goes on to say that to meet the needs of society to have "citizens who are not just literate but able to continuously learn and grow . . . learners need to be treated as individuals, with their needs, strengths, and weaknesses accounted for within the curriculum" (p. 41). Although instructors are seldom asked about how they would like their classrooms designed, those focused on promoting learning would agree with Cornell that the physical environment needs to be bigger, more flexible, provide ubiquitous access to technology, promote interaction and a sense of community, enable formal and informal learning, and convey a sense of energy. The environment should be a place people want to be, not just a place they have to be. They should be motivated by fun and enjoyment as much as by a desire to learn. (p. 41)

Problems that confront us when we use old-fashioned classrooms for twenty-first century teaching include room size, noise, temperature, lighting, technology, and seating. We all have had the experience, as teacher or student, of moving chairs and tables to make the setting more conducive to the type of activities in the course. Classrooms need to be a good match for the number of students in the course, the types of in-class learning experiences, rules for using the room (such as whether eating is allowed), and the room's general ambience. In addition, the instructor needs to be able to control the level of noise, temperature, and lighting and to adjust the seating in order to maximize learning experiences.

Teaching assistants can be another part of the classroom environment. Planning for having a TA or multiple TAs, depending on the number of students in the class, needs to receive your full attention. In some ways TAs are junior colleagues and you are their teaching mentor; in other ways, they are apprentice teachers and your regular meetings with them are equivalent to your facilitating a course on teaching and learning in your discipline. You, in turn, will learn a great deal from your TAs who are immersed in cutting-edge research in your field and also may be involved in TA training on the latest pedagogy. TAs, of course, have the same types of characteristics that you and your students do, including a variety of learning styles, as well as instructor characteristics, such as teaching styles.

When working with TAs, you need to take your managerial duties seriously. TAs usually are graduate students, but many colleges and universities have undergraduate TA programs. TAs are students first, and their time spent as TAs needs to be well structured so that it does not interfere with their studies. The better you know your TAs, the better you can help them learn to help your students, and you. Selecting, orienting, supervising, and evaluating TAs takes considera-

tion, professionalism, empathy, and time and needs to be included in your course design.

Having well-prepared TAs is very important when teaching large classes. Chism (1989) reports that faculty may not always agree on what is a large class, but researchers most often consider 100 or more students a large class. Interestingly, Wulff, Nyquist, and Abbott (1987) found that a majority of students set the number at 75 or more students. Rebecca Litke (1995) identifies three beliefs held by faculty about large classes:

1. *Increased class size means decreased student learning and satisfaction.* Although faculty hold this view, students report that "the quality of instruction, not size, determines how successful classes will be" (Wulff et al., 1987, p. 18) and students have a "basic view . . . that a good teacher can teach in any size class" (Litke, 1995, p. 114).
2. *Large classes cannot be taught like small classes.* Litke (1995) reports that although teaching large classes does require some modifications, the literature shows that "effective teaching and learning can occur in the large class" (p. 115).
3. *Student ratings of instructors are lower in large classes.* Wulff et al. (1987) reported that ratings of large-class instructors may be as high as small-class instructors and that "the best large classes can rival the best small classes on several instructional dimensions" (p. 27).

In Litke's (1995) study, students listed four categories in favor of large classes:

1. *Instructor Style,* including good clarity, interesting lectures, and active involvement in course;
2. *Use of Class Time,* including interesting content, guest speakers, and group activities;
3. *Group Interaction,* including a good climate of diversity and inquiry; and
4. *Individual Interaction,* including an attempt to use student names and student-related examples.

Students who did not like large classes were dissatisfied with the categories Use of Class Time, particularly wrong pace, and too much material and content; Group Interaction, such as poor class participation, lack of respect for classmates, and distractions; and Individual Interaction, such as a lack of attempt to personalize, low interest in students, and no attempt to use student names. In addition, they noted other factors such as previous negative experiences with a large class; and a poor environment, particularly bad acoustics.

Another consideration in designing your course is the technology available in your classroom. Each institution develops technology at its own pace and in its own order. Some institutions have provided access to the Internet in all classrooms but not provided a course management system such as Blackboard™. Others have provided all students with laptops or installed response systems (like the ones on the television show _Who Wants to Be a Millionaire?_) in large lecture halls. Classroom technology changes continually and needs to be considered in course design.

Notre Dame University proposed four recommendations for the design of learning spaces, which it defines as "any location where learning occurs. It is not necessarily limited to a classroom. It can also be a lab, a quad, a faculty office, or a student snack shop" (Laughner, 2003, p. 150). These recommendations are as follows:

- Use Learning Spaces to Increase Faculty-Student Interaction
  - improve opportunities for interaction between faculty and students in academic space
  - create social spaces in office and classroom area
  - provide seating outside of faculty offices so that students can sit comfortably while waiting to speak to their professors

- Design Classroom to Provide Maximum Classroom Flexibility
  - identify a campus advocate to study and recommend flexible and technology-enhanced learning spaces
- Design Guidelines to Assure Consistent Classroom Design
  - develop a model for technological implementation across campus
- Develop a Support Structure for Learning Spaces
  - develop a support model so that technology can be brought to any space
  - develop a process to assure class sessions are not lost if technology fails

(Laughner, 2003, pp. 151–152)

ONLINE ENVIRONMENT

Online environments vary according to the type of technology used and the technical support available. Some courses are taught entirely online, whereas others are "hybrid," including both face-to-face (f2f) time and online communication. The first question to ask yourself when planning to teach using the World Wide Web or a course management system, such as Blackboard or WebCT, is: How will the inclusion of technology help students better achieve their learning objectives?

Chapter 16 discusses teaching online in more depth. One big benefit of this method of teaching is that online systems provide an electronic bulletin board for students to post their own work and to respond to each other's work, allowing collaboration and practice in evaluation. There also are built-in management tools that assist in testing, recording grades, and providing quick feedback to students.

CHAPTER 6

Content

LEARNING OBJECTIVES

Readers of this chapter will be able to:

- Describe the design process from "the big questions" to teaching goals and learning objectives.
- Describe a Design Blueprint.
- Place learning objectives into Blueprint segments with their teaching goals.

FINALLY! HAVING CONSIDERED THE INSTRUCTOR, THE students, and the learning environment, it is time to consider the many possibilities for course content.

THE BIG QUESTIONS OR INTRIGUING PROBLEMS THAT YOUR COURSE WILL HELP STUDENTS CONFRONT, ANSWER, AND SOLVE

The extraordinary teachers in Ken Bain's (2004) study began their courses by describing to their students the "promises or opportunities the course offered . . . what the students would be doing to realize those promises (formerly known as requirements) . . . [and] how the instructor and students would understand the nature and progress of their learning" (p. 75). Their courses were designed so that "students encountered the information in the context of struggling, first with understanding and then with application of that comprehension" (p. 30). The questions they asked themselves and their students were "Why [would] anyone want to remember a particular piece of information?" "What does this fact help you understand? What problems does it help you address?" (p. 30).

What are the "big questions" that your course will

help students address? The outstanding teachers in the Bain (2004) study asked themselves: What reasoning abilities will the students need to succeed? What mental models will they bring with them? What information will the students need to understand in order to answer the important questions? What can I do to help students learn outside of class? How will I help students who have difficulty understanding? What stories can I tell them to help them connect with the material?

One of the factors that Bain (2004) found in the exceptional teachers was that they had an "unusually keen sense of the histories of their disciplines, including the controversies that have swirled within them" (p. 25). The controversies, of course, contain the big questions.

The exceptional teachers in Bain's study (2004) believed that "people learn best when they ask an important question that they care about answering, or adopt a goal that they want to reach. If they don't care, they will not try to reconcile, explain, modify, or integrate new knowledge with old" (p. 31). These instructors began designing each course by finding the "big questions" in their disciplines, the ones that had captured *their* interest as students and that might, in turn, capture the interest of their students. Each instructor began to design a course by thinking about the big questions in the discipline: What do you hope your students will understand after completing the course? Those might be the ideas and applications of your field that excite you, and that initially attracted *you* to your discipline. Why are you an economist? a journalist? a psychologist? a philosopher? a historian? How does your field affect society? individual achievement? the environment? Whatever your course, you have hopes that your students will appreciate the special qualities of the subject.

TEACHING GOALS

From your hopes, you will determine your teaching goals (TGs). Teaching goals belong to you, the instructor, not to your students. They are what *you* want to accomplish. There do not need to be "products" of TGs, so they do not have to be observable and measurable as they are in learning objectives (LOs). TGs allow you to aim for your students to "appreciate" something about your discipline and "understand" the significance of something substantive in your field. They are general plans such as "will learn the terms and facts of the subject." TGs are a commitment to teach and assess specific objectives but are not the objectives themselves. TGs lead directly to learning objectives.

LEARNING OBJECTIVES

Learning objectives (LOs) are the behaviors that students will be able to perform after completing the course. They are very specific and lead directly to the assessment of performance. LOs are the basis of the syllabus agreement. Professors must teach to every LO, provide modeling and feedback on student attempts to meet each one, as well as provide a rubric for how the LO will be assessed. This can be as simple as

"will be able to list the four main stages of historical development" being assessed by a test asking: "What are the four main stages of historical development?" It also can be as complicated as "will be able to apply Maslow's hierarchy to cases describing decisions about education" assessed by a 20-page research paper with a complex rubric for scoring. Learning objectives need to be concise, and teachable; result in an observable product (project, test, performance); and set at a single, appropriate level for the students and content. LOs are the centerpiece of course design. They are the basis for testing and for assessment rubrics. They determine whether or not you are a successful teacher, because your success will be demonstrated by your students' ability to achieve the learning objectives.

EFFICIENT DESIGN

Efficient design connects your teaching goals to your learning objectives, aids your choices of learning experiences (LEs), and leads directly to your evaluation plan (EP) for assessing your students' learning. As you will learn in section 2, it is necessary to place all four elements into the same developmental context. A Design Blueprint makes it easy to focus goals, objectives, experiences, and evaluation. The *Cognitive Taxonomy Design Blueprint* (Figure 6.1) is a matrix representing the two dimensions of the 2001 revision of Bloom's Taxonomy of Educational Objectives (Anderson & Krathwohl, 2001), which is described in detail in chapter 12. Each segment of the matrix demonstrates a type and level of development and has a place to describe a course TG, LO, LE, and EP. Segments are repeated for all elements that are at the same levels. Figure 6.2 is an example of segments for two different Bloom levels of TGs and LOs in an introductory psychology course.

Knowledge Dimension		Cognitive Process Dimension					
		TG = Teaching Goal LO = Learning Objective LE = Learning Experience EP = Evaluation Plan					
		1. Remember	2. Understand	3. Apply	4. Analyze	5. Evaluate	6. Create
A. Factual Knowledge	TG						
	LO						
	LE						
	EP						
B. Conceptual Knowledge	TG						
	LO						
	LE						
	EP						
C. Procedural Knowledge	TG						
	LO						
	LE						
	EP						
D. Meta-Cognitive Knowledge	TG						
	LO						
	LE						
	EP						

Figure 6.1   Cognitive Taxonomy Design Blueprint

Note. Laurie Richlin (2005), laurie.richlin@cgu.edu. Adapted from *Revised Bloom Taxonomy*, by J. McFann, 2005, presentation at the Southern California Professional Developers' Learning Community, Claremont, CA; and *A Taxonomy for Learning, Teaching, and Assessing: A Revision of Bloom's Taxonomy of Educational Objectives*, by L. W. Anderson and D. R. Krathwohl (Eds.), 2001, New York: Addison Wesley Longman.

Cognitive Taxonomy Design Blueprint

TG = Teaching Goal   LO = Learning Objective   LE = Learning Experience   EP = Evaluation Plan

Introductory Psychology Course

SEGMENT
Knowledge Dimension: Factual Knowledge
Cognitive Process: Remember

TG	Students will learn the facts and concepts of 20th-century psychology.
LO	Students completing this course will be able to list the five most influential psychologists of the 20th century.
LE	
EP	

SEGMENT
Knowledge Dimension: Conceptual Knowledge
Cognitive Process: Apply

TG	Students will understand how the psychological theories of the 20th century apply to current personal problems.
LO	Students completing this course will be able to apply concepts of 20th-century psychology to current personal problems.
LE	
EP	

As the course develops, the blueprint will include the learning experiences used to facilitate the students' learning and how that learning will be assessed in the evaluation plan.

Figure 6.2   Example Segments of a Course Design Blueprint

SECTION TWO

Facilitating Learning

THIS SECTION EXPLORES THEORIES ABOUT HOW PEOPLE, PARTICULARLY college students, learn. It explores ideas from neuroscience, psychology, and higher education, including the work of Zull on "changing the brain"; Gardner's Multiple Intelligences; the Kolb Experiential Learning Cycle; Bloom' cognitive, affective, and psychomotor taxonomies; Perry's and Belenkey, Clinchy, Goldberger, and Tarule's work on the cognitive development of college students; and the latest findings by Grasha and others on learning styles and motivation.

The various learning styles or intelligences help us to discover the different ways we and our students represent information in our minds. Knowing your own and your students' learning preferences enables you to orient the design of your course learning experiences most effectively. We begin with theories on our biologically based reactions to the environment, because they represent the way we most efficiently adopt data; learn; and, therefore, have the most impact on teaching and learning (Learnativity, 2002).

CHAPTER 7

Biology of Learning

LEARNING OBJECTIVES

Readers of this chapter will be able to:

- Define learning.
- Describe the physical changes involved in learning.
- Describe the different brain area functions.

IT IS ALL ABOUT LEARNING. EVERY ACTION WE TAKE AS instructors is based on our expectation that our students will be able to change something that they know, feel, or can do. Peter Beidler (1986), CASE Professor of the Year in 1983, writes, "Teaching is a complex art, if only because there is no teaching unless those being taught actually learn" (p. 51). Or, as Angelo and Cross (1993) say, "Teaching without learning is just talking" (p. 3). In their 15-year study, Ken Bain (2004) and colleagues found that the first question outstanding teachers ask themselves when they begin designing a course is: "What should my students be able to do intellectually, physically, or emotionally as a result of their learning?" (p. 49).

Learning happens and is seen on at least two levels: There are physical changes in the brain as a person is processing information and there is a potential change in behavior that the learner can perform. Because we do not have the opportunity to attach sensors to our students' brains while they are in our courses (although some professors are working on that), we rely on students' behaviors, such as how well they score on tests or how well they can paint, to signify learning. Biochemist Jim Zull, selected as 2001 Professor-of-the-Year by the Greek Life organizations at Case Western University, begins the introduction to his landmark book *The Art*

of Changing the Brain on the physical aspects of learning with the statement: "Learning is about biology" (Zull, 2002, p. xiii).

The most basic level of the brain is composed of cells, called neurons, that transmit information from one to an other through neural pathways. Neurons connect along a pathway called a synapse. Brains have about 100 billion neurons, with as many as 10,000 connections per neuron (Zull, 2002, p. 97). Zull (2002) writes, "The . . . thing we need to know about neurons for our immediate purposes is that they make friends easily. They form connections with other neurons" (p. 96). Furthermore, they make an effort to maintain those friendships. What your students "know" is in their already established neural pathways. There is no way to eradicate existing pathways; that is, when we tell students that what they know is "wrong," it does not weaken the relevant pathway. In fact, it strengthens the existing pathway because students use the existing pathway in recalling what is "wrong." For a pathway to fade, it must be unused. To learn correct information is to establish new, strong, used pathways. As an incorrect pathway is not used, it becomes weaker and the correct one is more likely to be the one called upon.

Neural pathways for different purposes are located in different areas of the brain. The top illustration in

Figure 7.1 is Zull's (2002) diagram of the left side of the cerebral cortex. The sensory portion in the back of the cortex is where signals from the eyes, ears, skin, mouth, and nose are received. The other areas are where the bulk of the neural pathways that integrate and create movement (motor) are located. The process is "Sense ➤ Integrate ➤ Act" (p. 15).

The lower illustration in Figure 7.1 demonstrates what Zull (2002) refers to as an oversimplified cycle of how we process information in different areas of the brain. He describes this cycle as follows:

> Sensory input could come from the outside world or from our own body, but once those signals have entered the sensory part of the cortex, they flow first through the integrative part of the brain nearest the sensory part, then through the integrative part nearest the motor brain, and then to the motor brain itself. Once action has been initiated, that action is detected by the sensory brain, so the output of the brain becomes new sensory input. (p. 16)

Zull relates the physical construction of the brain and the way the brain processes information to the Kolb Experiential Learning Cycle. We will consider that relationship after we explore the Kolb Cycle itself in the next chapter.

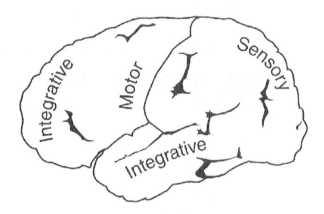

Zull, page 15

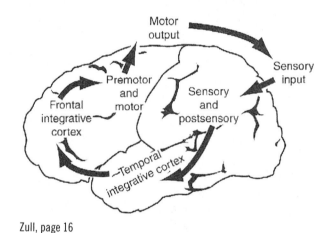

Zull, page 16

Figure 7.1. Brain Diagrams

Note. From *The Art of Changing the Brain: Enriching the Practice of Teaching by Exploring the Biology of Learning,* by J. E. Zull, 2002, Sterling, VA: Stylus. Copyright 2002 by Stylus. Reprinted with permission.

CHAPTER 8

Kolb Experiential Learning Cycle

LEARNING OBJECTIVES

Readers of this chapter will be able to:

- Describe the two continua of the cycle.
- Describe the activities of the four types of learning preferences.
- Describe the characteristics of the four types of learners.
- Describe how the cycle relates to brain structure.
- Describe types of learning experiences preferred by the different types of learners.

IN 1984, DAVID KOLB DEVELOPED A MODEL OF LEARN-
ing that has been used and modified by many educators to conceptualize how their students prefer to go
about learning. It is Kolb's assertion that each of us has
a preferred way to enter the cycle of learning. Think,
for instance, of being assigned the task of assembling
a doghouse. How would you go about it? Would you
take your time and read the instructions through until
you fully understand them? Would you grab your ham-
mer and get right to work, only looking at the manual
if you get into trouble? Perhaps you prefer to watch
someone else build a few doghouses together before you
attempt your own. Or, maybe you prefer to begin with
a deep understanding of the theories of doghouse archi-
tecture and construction. It is important to note that
to learn anything deeply we need to go fully around
the cycle, so we are talking only about our preferred
entry point. However, providing multiple entry points
for students to begin learning increases the likelihood
that they will engage the material.

The Kolb Experiential Learning Cycle, shown in
Figure 8.1, has two continua. The horizontal axis is the
Processing Continuum, which goes from "Active Exper-
imentation" (AE) to "Reflective Observation" (RO).
The vertical axis is the *Perception Continuum*, which
goes from "Concrete Experience" (CE) to "Abstract

Conceptualization" (AC). Kolb's *Learning Style Inventory*© provides 12 statements that describe different
ways of responding to classroom and day-to-day situations. For each statement, respondents choose which
answer is the first, second, third, and fourth most likely
action or feeling. The results of the inventory place
you in one of four quadrants, which represent different
learning cycle preferences.

If you are between AE and CE, you are termed an
Accommodator or activist. Accommodators prefer active experimentation, perform well in emergencies,
solve problems intuitively, and their greatest strength is
"doing things." If this is your style, you probably enjoy
carrying out plans and involving yourself in new and
challenging experiences. Your tendency may be to act
on subjective feelings, rather than on objective analysis.
In solving problems, you may rely more heavily on
other people for information than on your own inter-
nally derived analysis. This learning style is important
for effectiveness in action-oriented careers such as the
discipline of marketing.

If you are between CE and RO, you are termed a
Diverger or reflector. Divergers are good at generating
ideas and seeing things from different perspectives,
interested in people, prefer to watch rather than do,
gather information, and use imagination to solve

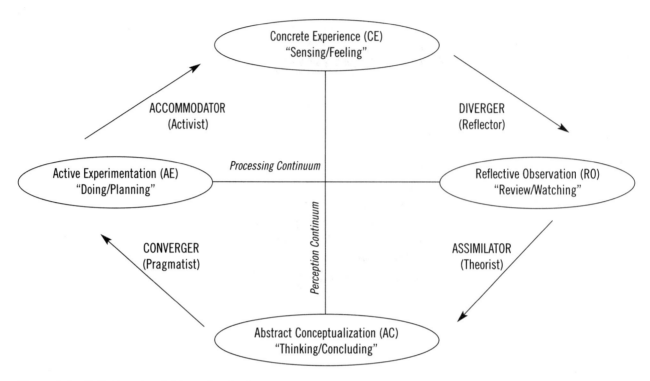

Figure 8.1   Kolb Experiential Learning Cycle

Note. From *Experiential Learning: Experience as the Source of Learning and Development,* by D. A. Kolb, 1984, Englewood Cliffs, NJ: Prentice-Hall; D. Clark, 1995, http://www.nwlink.com/~donclark/hrd/sat4.html; and "Accommodating Diverse Learning Styles: Designing Instruction for Electronic Information Sources," by M. E. Litzinger and B. Osif, 1993, in *What Is Good Instruction Now? Library Instruction for the 90s* (pp. 73–82), L. Shirato (Ed.), Ann Arbor, MI: Pierian Press. Adapted with permission.

problems. If this is your style, you may enjoy situations that call for generating a wide range of ideas, such as in brainstorming sessions. You probably have broad cultural interest and like to gather information. This imaginative ability and sensitivity to feelings is necessary for effectiveness in disciplines such as the arts, entertainment, and service careers.

If you are between RO and AC, you are termed an Assimilator or theorist. Assimilators excel in inductive reasoning, are concerned with abstract concepts rather than people, and have a strong ability to create theoretical models. If this is your learning style, you probably are less focused on people and more interested in abstract ideas and concepts. Generally, people with this learning style find it more important that a theory have logical soundness than practical value. This learning style is important for effectiveness in information and science careers.

If you are between AC and AE, you are termed a

Converger or pragmatist. Convergers can solve problems and will use learning to find solutions to practical issues, prefer technical tasks, are less concerned with people and interpersonal aspects, and are strong in the practical application of ideas. If this is your preferred learning style, you have the ability to solve problems and make decisions based on finding solutions to problems. You would rather deal with technical tasks and problems than with social and interpersonal issues. These learning skills are important for effectiveness in technology disciplines.

Different types of learning experiences appeal to the various Kolb styles. For instance, Concrete Experiencers prefer laboratories, fieldwork, and observation; Reflective Experiencers enjoy keeping logs and journals and brainstorming; Abstract Conceptualizers learn best from lectures, papers, and analogies; and Active Experimenters prefer simulations, case studies, and homework. As you can see in Figure 8.2, Zull (2002) has superimposed the Kolb cycle over his diagram of the brain, connecting each of the four categories to a particular brain site:

Concrete Experience ➤ Sensory and Postsensory
Reflective Observation ➤ Temporal Integrative Cortex
Abstract Conceptualization ➤ Frontal Integrative Cortex
Active Experimentation ➤ Premotor and Motor

Zull recounts his own "aha!" moment. As a new teaching center director he was pleased to have the opportunity to study "learning." When he discovered Kolb's book, he says, "It wasn't particularly about biology, but it still came closer to what interested me, so I plunged in" (p. 13). He reports

> I was skeptical of this idea at first. Surely there were many other ways to explain learning. It seemed too simple, too arbitrary. But I gave it a chance. And, without warning, as I sat in my office on one warm spring afternoon, it all came together. I still remember taking that slow, deep breath, holding it for a second, and then releasing it with a sound somewhere between a laugh and a sigh. I stood up and began to pace and talk to myself. "It's biological! Of course, it has to be. Everything in the right place! It's too pretty not to be true!" (p. 14)

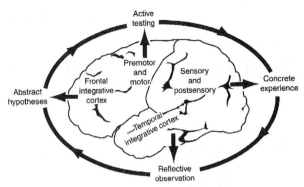

Zull, page 18

Figure 8.2   The Brain and the Kolb Experiential Learning Cycle

Note. From *The Art of Changing the Brain: Enriching the Practice of Teaching by Exploring the Biology of Learning*, by J. E. Zull, 2002, Sterling, VA: Stylus. Copyright 2002 by Stylus. Reprinted with permission. Note that Zull has rotated the Kolb Cycle 90° clockwise to match the brain areas responsible for each function.

Zull goes on to explain that in biology, function follows structure: "Any function found in any living organism must depend on some structure of some part of that organism" (p. 14). From there, he integrated what he knew about the biology of the brain with how Kolb describes the cycle of learning.

CHAPTER 9

Gardner's Multiple Intelligences

LEARNING OBJECTIVES

Readers of this chapter will be able to:

- Describe the nine types of Multiple Intelligences.
- Describe the impact of the MIs on education.
- Describe four types of mental content.
- Describe seven factors that can be used for learning.

HOWARD GARDNER IS BEST KNOWN FOR CHALLENGing the belief that intelligence is a singular attribute. He identified a series of "multiple intelligences" (MIs) that develop separately within our brains (Gardner, 1993). Each of the intelligences can be destroyed by injury without harming or changing the others, which accounts for individuals who can understand songs but have lost their ability to understand spoken words, or who can recognize symbols, such as the Coca Cola™ sign, but not the same words in writing. In the other direction, any of the intelligences can be highly developed, "genius," whereas the other intelligences are ordinary or even subordinary (e.g., the main characters in the films *Being There,* Peter Sellers; *Rain Man,* Dustin Hoffman; and *Forrest Gump,* Tom Hanks).

INTELLIGENCES OF THE SYMBOL ANALYST

Intelligences of the symbol analyst are what we often term *cognitive* abilities. Individuals usually are better at one of these than the other. They are particularly important for the types of schools (and tests) that we have.

1. Verbal-Linguistic Intelligence—spoken and written language; well-developed verbal skills; and sensitivity to the sounds, meanings, and rhythms of words
2. Mathematical-Logical Intelligence—ability to think conceptually and abstractly, and the capacity to discern logical or numerical patterns

"NONCANONICAL" INTELLIGENCES

Noncanonical intelligences are additional forms of mental representations, not as applicable to our school systems, but of greater importance in other times and cultures. They range across cognitive, affective, and psychomotor abilities.

3. Musical Intelligence—sensitivity to the perception and production of music, analogous to linguistic intelligence; ability to produce and appreciate rhythm, pitch, and timber (includes cognitive, affective, and psychomotor abilities)
4. Visual-Spatial Intelligence—capacity to think in images and pictures, to visualize accurately and abstractly (mostly cognitive)

5. Bodily-Kinesthetic Intelligence—ability to control one's body movements and/or to handle objects skillfully (psychomotor)
6. Naturalistic Intelligence—ability to make consequential discriminations in the natural world, that is, to recognize and categorize plants, animals, and other objects in nature; and to discriminate among consumer objects in the urban world (cognitive and affective)

PERSONAL INTELLIGENCES

Personal intelligences are cognitive and affective abilities having to do with understanding ourselves, others, and philosophical meaning.

7. Intrapersonal Intelligence—capacity to be self-aware and in tune with inner feelings, values, beliefs, and thinking processes; important in connected knowing
8. Interpersonal Intelligence—capacity to detect and respond appropriately to the moods, motivations, and desires of others
9. Existential Intelligence—ability to ponder deep questions about human existence, such as the meaning of life, why we die, how we got here; important in critical and creative thinking

IMPACT OF MULTIPLE INTELLIGENCES ON EDUCATION

The Western education system is based on developing mathematical and linguistic intelligences. We are so committed to those intelligences that students who do not achieve a certain level of success in them are not allowed to participate in activities using intelligences at which they *do* excel. Think, for instance, about policies stating that students who do not receive at least a C in mathematics and English courses are not allowed to play in the band, which uses musical intelligence, or on a sports team, which uses kinesthetic intelligence. If students are allowed to use their preferred intelligences to learn and explain concepts, they have a better chance of grasping the material.

The educational impact of considering the multiple intelligences for learning has been primarily at the grammar school level, where statewide (e.g., Kentucky), districtwide, and school (e.g., Key School in Indianapolis) plans have been developed to educate each of the intelligences each day. Higher education has been slower to incorporate MI theory. It has been used by individual professors to allow students to express ideas in different ways. For instance, Milton Cox has his calculus students at Miami University choose a nonmathematical intelligence to express the theory of "limit." Students compose poems, write songs, and draw pictures. Figure 9.1 is a student poster presentation titled "A Kiss," along with the student's explanation of its relationship to the theory.

MENTAL CONTENT

In his recent book, Gardner (2004) calls learning "a change of mind." Tying in with what we have heard from Zull, Gardner writes, "On the most basic level, a change of mind involves a change of mental representation" (p. 30). He identifies four types of mental content:

A concept, which is "an umbrella term that refers to any set of closely related entities" (p. 19)
Stories, which are "narratives that describe events that unfold over time" (p. 19)
Theories, which are "relatively formal explanations of processes in the world" (p. 19–20)
Skills, which "consist of procedures that individuals know how to carry out, whether or not they choose to—or even can—put them into words" (pp. 20–21)

LEVERS TO CHANGE MINDS

The fact that mental representation changes is, of course, very good news for teachers, whose work is changing minds. Along this line, Gardner (2004) identifies seven factors or "levers" that can be used to change minds (p. 33).

    For the section where we must choose an intelligence
other than mathematical/logical to understand and explain
the limit concept, I chose to use the visual/spatial
intelligence. While looking through a magazine, my head was
swimming with ideas, until I stumbled upon an idea that made
me think of the limit. This is what I did...

    I saw a picture of a man and a woman kissing, and they
had "limit" written all over their faces. I thought of how
people actually kiss, and I envisioned the two people moving
closer from two different directions that finally come
together at a single point.

    How I incorporated this to the limit concept was by
using the "left-hand" and "right-hand" limit. The man is
approaching a point "a" (which is directly above the letter
A) from the left-hand side, and the woman is moving to "a"
from the right-hand side. An equation would look somewhat
like this:

$$\lim_{x \to a^-} f(x) = kiss \quad (man)$$

$$\lim_{x \to a^+} f(x) = kiss \quad (woman)$$

Figure 9.1   Demonstration of the "Theory of Limit" in Calculus in a Gardner Non-mathematical Intelligence.

Milton D. Cox (1998). Used by permission.

reason, a rational approach (p. 15);

research, a collection of relevant data (from a database or experience) (p. 15);

resonance, an affective "fit" (p. 15);

redescriptions, where a variety of mental forms reinforce the change (p. 16);

resources and rewards, positive reinforcement that will work only if the mind change matches with other criteria (p. 16);

real world events, which affect many people (p. 17);

and, in opposition to changing, *resistances*, which are ideas developed and entrenched over time (pp. 17–18)

All of these come into play when designing a course. From Zull we know that the entrenched ideas are, of course, the neural pathways that have been used in the past. And the levers are part of the experiences that will forge learning.

CHAPTER 10

Styles of Learning and Teaching

LEARNING OBJECTIVES

Readers of this chapter will be able to:

- List student descriptors of outstanding professors.
- Describe student perceptions of ineffective professors.
- Describe six learning styles and their classroom preferences.
- Describe five teaching styles and their advantages and disadvantages.
- Describe how the learning styles and teaching styles combine into four clusters and the associated teaching methods.
- Demonstrate learning diversity in a class session by constructing an instructional script.

ALTHOUGH THE MESSINESS OF TEACHING AND LEARNing leads to excitement and variety in each teaching situation, it also means that there are multiple elements to consider when designing any course, even one that has been taught many times before. Individuals' comfort level with teaching is as complex as how they learn.

In Bain's (2004) study, the exceptional teachers realized that understanding changes slowly, and that "to accomplish that feat, learners must (1) face a situation in which their mental model will not work (that is, will not help them explain or do something); (2) care that it does not work strongly enough to stop and grapple with the issue at hand; and (3) be able to handle the emotional trauma that sometimes accompanies challenges to longstanding beliefs" (pp. 27–28). The outstanding teachers had a "much richer line of inquiry [than other teachers] to design a class, lecture, discussion section, clerkship, or any other encounter with students, and they begin with questions about student learning objectives rather than about what the teaching will do" (p. 17).

Each teaching style translates into modes of behavior that include communication elements such as speaking, listening, gestures, movements, and responding. Joe Lowman (1994, 1995) conducted several studies on behaviors that students identified in

outstanding teachers, using both surveys and the letters that the students wrote nominating teachers for awards. The students' descriptors, shown in Figure 10.1, fall into two categories: intellectual excitement and interpersonal rapport. In other words, students want professors who are knowledgeable and excited about the material and who care about their learning. Also, notice the effective motivation descriptors in Figure 10.1, which include both "challenging" and "encouraging."

On the other side, Barbara Carson (1999) has identified traits of ineffective professors. More than 200 college students who graduated between 1964 and 1990 responded to Carson's request for narratives about their least effective teachers. She found three main factors that provide almost perfect counterpoint to Lowman's outstanding teachers' behaviors: Ineffective teachers "lack passion for subject matter," are unable to "connect students and subject matter," and display "indifference or hostility toward students" (1999, p. 95). Figure 10.2 shows the specific behaviors and attitudes that are included in each factor.

Tony Grasha (1972) became fascinated by variations in the ways students worked with their peers and the teacher in the classroom. In collaboration with Sheryl Hruska-Riechmann, he developed an inventory

Intellectual Excitement	
Enthusiastic	Exciting
Knowledgeable	Engaging
Inspiring	Prepared
Humorous	Energetic
Interesting	Fun
Clear	Stimulating
Organized	Eloquent
Creative	Communicative

Interpersonal Rapport	
Interpersonal Concern	*Effective Motivation*
Concerned	Helpful
Caring	Encouraging
Available	Challenging
Friendly	Fair
Accessible	Demanding
Approachable	Patient
Interested	Motivating
Respectful	
Understanding	
Personable	

Figure 10.1   Classification of Student Descriptors of Classroom Behaviors of Outstanding Instructors

Note. From *Teaching with Style: A Practical Guide to Enhancing Learning by Understanding Teaching & Learning Styles,* p. 4, by A. F. Grasha, 1996, Claremont, CA: Alliance (www.iats.com). Based on information from J. Lowman, 1994, "Professors as Performers and Motivators," *College Teaching, 42,* 137–141. Used by permission.

to identify and categorize student learning behavior preferences. They categorized these as Avoidant, Dependent, Participant, Independent, Competitive, and Collaborative. Figure 10.3 presents a description of each style and the general classroom learning experiences (LEs) preferred by each type of student.

The *Grasha-Riechmann Student Learning Style Scales Inventory* (pp. 126–128) has been used in higher education and other educational settings for more than three decades. Inventories from several thousand students have been used to describe the distribution of learning styles across the categories major, graduate/undergraduate, type of institution, sex, age, and grades (Grasha, 1996). Grasha found no significant difference in learning styles among majors or between graduate and undergraduate students. Students in two-year, particularly technical schools tend to be

more dependent, competitive, and participatory than students in four-year schools. Several differences are reported between men and women: Women in undergraduate, liberal arts majors score higher in collaboration; men in physical education are more competitive, avoidant, and independent; and female nurses are more dependent and participatory than male nurses. Students over the age of 25 tend to be more independent and participatory in their learning styles; those under 25 display higher levels of avoidance and competitiveness and lower levels of participation in the classroom. Students with an Avoidant style achieve lower grades and those with a Participant style achieve higher ones.

Of course, people do not have only one style that they use at all times and in all situations. Everyone is a blend of styles and we use them selectively, often based on our motivation and interest. Students who sit passively (or sleep) through one course can be seen enthusiastically participating in a different one. Students who are silent in class can participate actively in discussions outside of class. A study comparing Grasha learning styles in matched classroom and online courses (Diaz & Cartnal, n.d.) found that students in the online course had higher independent and lower dependent scores, which would be expected because they self-selected for the type of course. They also were less collaborative, although they were willing to collaborate through teacher-directed assignments. Students in the on-campus class were significantly more dependent than those in the on-line course.

After 25 years of using his Learning Styles Inventory (LSI), Grasha became dissatisfied with the various ways teaching styles were modeled. In 1988, he began a program of research to develop an integrated model of teaching and learning styles. Grasha (1996) states, *"My goals were to describe the stylistic qualities of teachers and students, to show how they related to each other, and to offer suggestions for how this information could be used to enhance the nature and quality of classroom experiences"* (p. 152, italics in original). The Grasha Teaching Styles Inventory (TSI) (found in section 5) is a series of 40 questions that result in five teaching styles: Expert, Formal Authority, Personal Model, Facilitator, and Delegator. Just as with learning styles, no one is purely one type, but a mix. Professors studied by Grasha reported using the Expert and Formal Authority styles more with their freshmen and sophomores,

Ineffective Professors: Negative Variables Reported by Students	
Students' Perception of Professor	*Behavior/Attitudes Reported*
Lack of Passion for Subject Matter	• Absence of energy, enthusiasm, inspiration • Lack of interest in the subject • Lack of attention to method of presentation • Monotonic voice • Teaching from textbook • Low standards for self and for students
Inability to Connect Students and Subject Matter	• Greater concern for subject than for students' learning • Lack of organization • Lack of clarity in explaining course content • Absence of pedagogical variety • Failure to stimulate student involvement • Failure to connect abstraction and theory to practice and life
Indifference or Hostility Toward Students	• Lack of concern and respect for students • Inaccessibility, both figurative and literal • Lack of interest in students as individuals • Lack of encouragement • Use of fear, embarrassment, belittlement as motivators • Favoritism • Unclear, unreasonable, arbitrary grading system • False accusations of academic dishonesty • Breaches of professional behavior (inappropriate friendships, inappropriate displays of personal problems, sexism, sexual harassment

Figure 10.2   Traits of Ineffective Professors Identified by More Than 200 College Students Who Graduated between 1964 and 1990

Note. From "Bad News in the Service of Good Teaching: Students Remember Ineffective Professors," by B. H. Carson, 1999, *Journal on Excellence in College Teaching,* *10*(1), p. 95. Copyright 2000, JECT. Used by permission.

less with their juniors and seniors, and even less with their graduate students. By contrast, Delegator and Facilitator styles were used less at the lower levels and more at the higher. Figure 10.4 provides a full description of each style.

As Grasha planned, the TSI and LSI interact. Figure 10.5 shows four clusters of teaching styles and learning styles and the learning experiences associated with each. In Cluster 1, Expert/Formal Authority teachers match with Independent/Participant/Competitive learners who prefer traditional learning experiences, such as lectures and technology-based presentations. In Cluster 2, the primary teaching styles are Personal Model/Expert/Formal Authority, matched with Participant/Dependent/Competitive students who prefer role modeling, coaching, and guiding. In Cluster 3, Facilitator/Personal Model/Expert teachers match

with Collaborative/Participant/Independent students who prefer very active learning experiences, such as case studies, role plays, fishbowl discussions, and problem-based learning. In Cluster 4, Delegator/Facilitator/Expert teachers match with Independent/Collaborative/Participant students and use the loosest type of learning experiences, such as contract teaching, independent study, and self-discovery activities.

A useful way to use the LSI/TSI clusters is by designing what Grasha calls an *instructional script*. Figure 10.6 provides an example from a psychology course of a script for a 90-minute class session (a blank script is provided in section 5). The instructor's name, course, and specific learning objectives for the session go at the top of the script. The first column, "Time Line," shows how many minutes the instructor

Learning Style	*General Classroom Preferences*
Avoidant Not enthusiastic about learning content and attending class. Do not participate with students and teachers in the classroom. They are uninterested and overwhelmed by what goes on in class.	Generally turned off by most classroom activities Would prefer no tests Pass-fail grading systems Does not like enthusiastic teachers Does not want to be called on in class
Dependent Show little intellectual curiosity and who learn only what is required. View teacher and peers as sources of structure and support and look to authority figures for specific guidelines on what to do.	Outlines or notes on the board Clear deadlines and instructions for assignments Teacher-centered classroom methods As little ambiguity as possible in all aspects of course
Participant Good citizens in class. Enjoy going to class and take part in as much of the course activities as possible. Typically eager to do as much of the required and optional course requirements as they can.	Lectures with discussion Opportunities to discuss material Class reading assignments Teachers who can analyze and synthesize information well
Independent Students who like to think for themselves and are confident in their learning abilities. Prefer to learn the content that they feel is important and would prefer to work alone on course projects than with other students.	Independent study Self-paced instruction Assignments that give students a chance to think independently Projects that student can design Student-centered rather than teacher-centered course designs
Competitive Students who learn material in order to perform better than others in the class. Believe they must compete with other students in a course for the rewards that are offered. Like to be the center of attention and to receive recognition for their accomplishments in class.	Become a group leader in discussions Teacher-centered instructional procedures Singled out in class for doing a good job Class activities where they can do better than others
Collaborative Typical of students who feel they can learn by sharing ideas and talents. They cooperate with teachers and like to work with others.	Lectures with small group discussions Small seminars Student-designed aspects of course Group projects

Figure 10.3   Grasha Learning Styles Descriptions and Classroom Preferences

plans for each content area, which is described in the second column. The "Stage Directions" column describes what the instructor will be doing in each segment, followed by the type of learning experiences involved. The "Diversity Check" column ties the learning experiences to a particular cluster of teaching styles and learning styles. The final two columns provide a reminder to the instructor about necessary materials and audiovisual (A/V) equipment required for the learning experiences.

Teaching Style	Advantage/Disadvantage
Expert Possesses knowledge and expertise that students need. Strives to maintain status as an expert among students by displaying detailed knowledge and by challenging students to enhance their competence. Concerned with transmitting information and insuring that students are well prepared.	**Advantage** The information, knowledge and skills such individuals possess. **Disadvantage** If overused, the display of knowledge can be intimidating to less experienced individuals. May not show the underlying thought processes that produced answers.
Formal Authority Possesses status among students because of knowledge and role as a faculty member. Concerned with providing positive and negative feedback, establishing learning goals, expectations, and rules of conduct for students. Concerned with the correct, acceptable, and standard ways to do things and with providing students with the structure they need to learn.	**Advantage** The focus on clear expectations and acceptable ways of doing things. **Disadvantage** A strong investment in this style can lead to rigid, standardized, and less flexible ways of managing students and their concerns.
Personal Model Believes in "teaching by personal example" and establishes a prototype for how to think and behave. Oversees, guides, and directs by showing how to do things, and encouraging students to observe and then to emulate the instructor's approach.	**Advantage** An emphasis on direct observation and following a role model. **Disadvantage** Some teachers may believe their approach is the best way, leading some students to feel inadequate if they cannot live up to such expectations and standards.
Facilitator Emphasizes the personal nature of teacher-student interactions. Guides and directs students by asking questions, exploring options, suggesting alternatives, and encouraging them to develop criteria to make informed choices. Overall goal is to develop in students the capacity for independent action, initiative, and responsibility. Works with students on projects in a consultative fashion and tries to provide as much support and encouragement as possible.	**Advantage** The personal flexibility, the focus on students' needs and goals, and the willingness to explore options and alternative courses of action. **Disadvantage** Style is often time consuming, and is sometimes employed when a more direct approach is needed. Can make students uncomfortable if it is not used in a positive and affirming manner.
Delegator Concerned with developing students' capacity to function in an autonomous fashion. Students work independently on projects or as part of autonomous teams. The teacher is available at the request of students as a resource person.	**Advantage** Helps students to perceive themselves as independent learners. **Disadvantage** May misread student's readiness for independent work. Some students may become anxious when given autonomy.

Figure 10.4   Grasha Teaching Styles Descriptions and Advantages/Disadvantages

Learning Experiences Associated with Each Cluster of Teaching and Learning Styles	
Cluster 1	**Cluster 2**

Primary Teaching Styles
    Expert/Formal Authority
Primary Learning Style
    Dependent/Participant/Competitive
	Primary Teaching Styles
	    Personal Model/Expert/Formal Authority
	Primary Learning Style
	    Participant/Dependent/Competitive

• Exams/Grades Emphasized
• Guest Speakers/Guest Interviews
• Lectures
• Mini-Lectures + Triggers
• Teacher-Centered Questioning
• Teacher-Centered Discussions
• Term Papers
• Tutorials
• Technology-Based Presentations
	• Role Playing by Illustration
	    ○ Discussing Alternative Approaches
	    ○ Sharing Thought Processes Involved in Obtaining Answers
	    ○ Sharing Personal Experiences
	• Role Modeling by Direct Action
	    ○ Demonstrating Way of Thinking/Doing Things
	    ○ Having Students Emulate Teacher
	• Coaching/Guiding Students

Cluster 3	**Cluster 4**

Primary Teaching Styles
    Facilitator/Personal Model/Expert
Primary Learning Style
    Collaborative/Participant/Independent
	Primary Teaching Styles
	    Delegator/Facilitator/Expert
	Primary Learning Style
	    Independent/Collaborative/Participant

• Case Studies
• Cognitive Map Discussion
• Critical Thinking Discussion
• Fishbowl Discussion
• Guided Readings
• Key Statement Discussions
• Kineposium
• Laboratory Projects
• Problem-Based Learning
    ○ Group Inquiry
    ○ Guided Design
    ○ Problem-Based Tutorials
• Role Plays/Simulations
• Roundtable Discussion
• Student Teacher of the Day
	• Contract Teaching
	• Class Symposium
	• Debate Formats
	• Helping Trios
	• Independent Study/Research
	• Jigsaw Groups
	• Laundry List Discussions
	• Modular Instruction
	• Panel Discussion
	• Learning Pairs
	• Position Papers
	• Practicum
	• Round Robin Interviews
	• Self-Discovery Activities
	• Small Group Work Teams
	• Student Journals

Figure 10.5   Four Clusters of Teaching Styles with Associated Learning Styles and Learning Experiences Identified by Grasha

Note. From *Teaching with Style: A Practical Guide to Enhancing Learning by Understanding Teaching and Learning Styles*, p. 234, by A. F. Grasha, 1996, Claremont, CA: Alliance Publishers (www.iats.com). Copyright 1995 by publisher. Reprinted with permission.

Instructor: Kimberly Cox Course: Introduction to Psychology						
Session Learning Objectives. *Students completing this session will be able to:* 1. *Define terminology of learning theory* 2. *Describe principles of learning theory* 3. *Describe Pavlov's experiment and results*						
Time Line	**Content**	**Stage Directions**	**Learning Experiences**	**Diversity Check**	**Materials**	**A/V**
15 minutes	Learning Theory	Move around to each small group.	key statement discussion—share discussion questions	Cluster 3	list of questions	
15 minutes	Principles and Terminology of Learning Theory	PowerPoint presentation Stand at front of room.	mini-lecture teacher-centered questioning technology-based presentation	Cluster 1		PowerPoint disk LCD projector
20 minutes	Pavlov's Experiment	Ask class to take notes on video. Sit with class.	technology-based presentation	Cluster 1		video VCR
10 minutes	Pavlov's Experiment	Stand at overhead.	computer simulation from the Nobel Prize Foundation	Cluster 3		computer and Internet connection
30 minutes	Learning Theory Concepts	Hand out exercises. Move around classroom to work with each group.	learning pairs (20 minutes) pairs share with class (10 minutes)	Cluster 4	handouts	

Figure 10.6   Sample Instructional Script

Source: Adapted from Kimberly Cox, 2002, classroom presentation. Used by permission.

CHAPTER 11

Cognitive Development Of College Students

LEARNING OBJECTIVES

Readers of this chapter will be able to:

- Define the cognitive perspective on learning.
- Describe the characteristics of the four major stages of the Perry Scheme.
- Describe the characteristics of the perspectives reported in *Women's Ways of Knowing.*

COGNITIVE DEVELOPMENT IS THE PROGRESS OF LEARN-ers from simple to more complicated schemes of knowing. Gardner (2004) describes the cognitive perspective as

> based on emerging scientific understanding of how the mind works, courtesy of psychology, neuroscience, linguistics, and other neighboring disciplines. It takes into account our inborn or early representations, and it acknowledges their debt to both cultural and biological factors. But most mental representations are neither given at birth nor frozen at the time of their adoption. In our terms, they are constructed over time within our mind/brains and they can be reformed, refashioned, reconstructed, transformed, combined, altered, and undermined. They are, in short, within our hands and within our minds. Mental representations are *not* immutable; analysis or reflective individuals are able to lay them out, and, while altering representations may not be easy, changes can be effected. Moreover, because we have at our disposal so many mental representations that can be combined in so many ways, the possibilities are essentially limitless. (p. 46)

Course design must take into consideration the developmental stages of our students and provide opportunities for students to move into more complex ways of knowing.

THE PERRY SCHEME

In the early 1950s, William Perry, a professor of English at Harvard University, became an academic advisor. Over the course of the following decade, he realized that first-year students asked different questions about their class work than sophomores, that sophomores asked different questions than juniors, and that juniors asked different questions than seniors. He categorized those questions, demonstrating how each group thought about knowledge and, thereby, how they viewed their job as students, and how they viewed professors and peers in the classroom. His landmark work, first published in 1968, presents a scheme of intellectual development composed of four main stages with many subcategories. Perry set out what he considered the "normal" steps in sequence, although he based his work on 140 traditional-aged students (28 women and 112 men) whom he interviewed at the end of each of the four years they attended Harvard. To clarify the

Stage	View of Knowledge	View of Professor	View of Peers
1. Dualism Students think that Knowledge is "out there," teachers have it, and the students' job is to get it from the instructors.	Absolute Received Black vs. White Right vs. Wrong	Expert Dispenser of Truth Should just provide the answers	Rejected They do not have expert Knowledge
Indication of Change to Multiplicity: acceptance of multiple views, some ambiguity			
2. Multiplicity Students begin to be uncertain. Since experts don't have the answers, they think that they can accept whatever each source says even if the opinions are contradictory.	Knowledge is a matter of opinion. All opinions are equal.	Not an authority Just another opinion	Just another opinion
Indication of Change to Relativism: able to back up opinions, argue, consider alternatives			
3. Relativism Students realize they have to make decisions on what to believe.	Contextual Complex Quality of knowledge	A resource to help learn methods of analysis	A legitimate source of knowledge
Indication of Change to Commitment: creation of a personal world view			
4. Commitment Initial commitment in some important aspect of life. Emergence of additional commitments. Commitments seen as ongoing activities. Sense of self as a source of knowledge, authority figure to self.	Knowledge intrinsic Convinced of knowledge	Not an absolute authority A resource A colleague	A legitimate source of knowledge

Figure 11.1   Characteristics of Perry Scheme of Cognitive Development Stages

Source: Adapted from Bettina Casad, 2002, classroom presentation. Used by permission.

categories in his study he based most of his conclusions on the reports of the male students (Perry, 1968/1970).

The Perry Scheme is easy to work with and explains a great deal about what we see in student learning behaviors. Figure 11.1 describes characteristics of the stages Dualism, Multiplicity, Relativism, and Commitment. As students develop, they move from seeing "knowledge" as something that teachers have and they need to "get," through confusion about what to believe, to a commitment to how they will judge evidence for making decisions.

It is my contention that we all go through the Perry steps every time we confront a new subject. Although we may have achieved Commitment in how we value evidence in one area, we usually begin as a Dualist in a new area. It does become easier to move through the stages each time. Of course, these stages do not relate only to schoolwork. Think, for instance, of a decision you have had to make recently. Each time you have had

to make a choice, such as in the purchase of a notebook computer (Mac or PC?), a car (sedan or SUV?), or a house (lots of choices), you have probably gone through the same process. In each case a person begins as a dualist believing (hoping) that there is an official answer, tries not to have to learn an entire new subject to make a decision, and wants to be given the correct answer by an expert. Furthermore, in each case it is likely that the choice will need to be based on the information available, and decided on personal criteria.

WOMEN'S WAYS OF KNOWING

Blythe Clinchy and Claire Zimmerman, working with female students at Wellesley College in the 1980s, attempted to "flesh out" the Perry Scheme, which they saw as a "sketchy outline of development" (Clinchy, 1990, p. 54). Although they expected and, indeed, ini-

Perspective	Characteristics
Silence	Signifies the voicelessness of women. These women have difficulty hearing as well as speaking. Silence grows out of a background of poverty, isolation, subordination, rejection, and often, violence. This is not a step in normal development but a failure to develop.
Received Knowing	Truth is absolute and unambiguous. Received knowers believe that for every question there is a correct answer. There is no room for ambiguity. Equivalent to Perry's position of Dualism.
Subjective Knowing	In some respects, the opposite of Received Knowledge. Deeply suspicious of information dispensed by others. Subjectivists look inside themselves for knowledge. Intuitionism. Similar to Perry's position of Multiplicity.
Procedural Knowing	No longer believe that one can acquire knowledge through immediate apprehension. Knowledge is a process. **Separate Knowing**: Implies a separation from the object of knowledge and mastery over it. Use of impersonal logical rules. Conforming to the demands of an external authority. / **Connected Knowing**: Builds on the subjectivists' conviction that the most trustworthy knowledge comes from personal experience rather than the pronouncements of authorities.
Constructed Knowing	All knowledge is constructed, and the knower is an intimate part of the known. Women weave together the strands of rational and emotive thought and integrate objective and subjective knowing. Question posing is central to the constructivist way of knowing.

Figure 11.2   Characteristics of Perspectives of *Women's Ways of Knowing*

Source: Adapted from Shannon Hensley, 2003, classroom presentation. Used by permission.

tially coded their students' responses into the Perry categories, Clinchy reports that "we accumulated an ugly pile of transcripts—we called them 'anomalies'—that refused to be wedged into the scheme. What they said just didn't seem relevant. So we left them out" (p. 55). Putting the students in the Perry Scheme seemed to work until the students were ready to leave multiplicity. At that point in Perry's (1968/1970) study, the male students learned that they needed to use analytical techniques to work with the disciplinary material. Clinchy (1990) reports that most of the female participants in her study learned to use analytical techniques,

but they did not then adopt those techniques as their "way of knowing." Instead, Clinchy reports that "they remained frozen in a schoolgirl mode, performing the cognitive tasks they were ordered to perform, often with considerable skill, but without joy or conviction and sometimes, ultimately, with despair" (p. 56).

At this point, Clinchy joined with Mary Belenky, Nancy Goldberger, and Jill Tarule, developmental psychologists from other institutions, in a national project that resulted in their book, *Women's Ways of Knowing* (Belenky, Clinchy, Goldberger, & Tarule, 1986). They interviewed 145 women in different types of colleges and from social agencies concerned with maternal and child health. Although they again tried to classify the responses into categories of the Perry Scheme, they found other descriptions more appropriate. Figure 11.2 describes what the researchers came to call "epistemological positions," how an individual develops conceptions of knowledge and knowing and then uses them to understand the world.

The female participants in the study went through five stages: Silence, Received Knowing, Subjective Knowing, Procedural Knowing, and Constructed Knowing. "Silence" and "Subjective Knowing" have no counterparts in the Perry Scheme and seem to be particular to women. *Silence* is a "pre-knowledge" state, representing a failure to develop. *Subjective Knowing* represents a suspicion of outside knowledge. Received Knowing is a counterpart to Perry's Dualism. *Procedural Knowing* has two parts: Separate Knowing and Connected Knowing. *Separate Knowing* requires the typical scientific distance, while *Connected Knowing* brings learners' subjective personal experiences into understanding. The final position, *Constructed Knowing,* blends both the rational (separate) and subjective.

The course design lesson of both the Perry (1968/ 1970) and Belenky et al. (1986) schemes is that it is difficult for students to move along the developmental stages. The challenge is to find ways to enable students to move to more advanced stages as quickly as possible. Robert Kloss (1994), in his article "A Nudge Is Best: Helping Students through the Perry Scheme of Intellectual Development," adds the important emotional component for critical thinking:

> We who have chosen to make our life's work the growth of others would do well to recall that literal biological growth occurs willy-nilly. No redwood resists becoming gigantic. But we have all repeatedly witnessed students resist learning, refusing—it would appear—to grow. The biological metaphor applied to education cannot adequately account for the complexity of our species. We must keep in mind that we are asking students to exit voluntarily an idyllic life of certainty where the locus of authority is clear—a Garden of Eden—and to assume the heavy burden of remaking the world anew day after day, a Sisyphean task at best. If we remember this, we will have a better perspective on how drastically uneven and unfair an exchange it may seem to them, and we can understand better the wisdom of their resistance. (p. 158)

CHAPTER 12

Bloom Taxonomies

LEARNING OBJECTIVES

Readers of this chapter will be able to:

- Describe the three Bloom taxonomies.
- Describe the two dimensions of the revised cognitive taxonomy.
- Describe two models of development along the process dimension of the revised cognitive taxonomy.
- Explain the importance of the verbs associated with each of the taxonomies.
- Design their course based on the Bloom taxonomies.

A COMMITTEE OF EDUCATIONAL PSYCHOLOGISTS WAS formed after the 1948 Convention of the American Psychological Association to develop a classification system for levels of intellectual behaviors. Chaired by Benjamin Bloom, the group eventually created three taxonomies.

COGNITIVE TAXONOMY

In 1956, Bloom and Krathwohl published a taxonomy of cognitive educational objectives. The most recent revision of the cognitive taxonomy was done by Anderson and Krathwohl in 2001. They divided the Cognitive taxonomy into Cognitive Process and Knowledge Dimensions that form a matrix of development in factual, conceptual, procedural, and meta-cognitive knowledge. Figures 12.1, 12.2, and 12.3 demonstrate how the dimensions relate to each other and describe the individual scales, including key verbs that can be used to design learning objectives. In this taxonomy, learners develop from simply remembering factual knowledge to being able to create new knowledge and reflect on their own learning.

Cognitive Process Dimension						
Knowledge Dimension	1. Remember	2. Understand	3. Apply	4. Analyze	5. Evaluate	6. Create
A. Factual Knowledge						
B. Conceptual Knowledge						
C. Procedural Knowledge						
D. Meta-Cognitive Knowledge						

Figure 12.1 Chart of Revised Bloom Cognitive Taxonomy

Note. From *A Taxonomy for Learning, Teaching, and Assessing: A Revision of Bloom's Taxonomy of Educational Objectives* by L. W. Anderson and D. R. Krathwohl, 2001, New York. Copyright 2001 by Addison Wesley Longman. Used by permission.

Knowledge Dimension	
A. Factual Knowledge: The basic elements students must know to be acquainted with a discipline or solve problems in it. Example verbs: *define, identify, list, name, recall, recognize*	
A1. Knowledge of terminology A2. Knowledge of specific details and elements	Technical vocabulary, musical symbols Major natural resources

B. Conceptual Knowledge: The interrelationships among the basic elements within a larger structure that enable them to function together. Example verbs: *describe, discuss, explain, express, interpret*	
B1. Knowledge of classifications and categories B2. Knowledge of principles and generalizations B3. Knowledge of theories, models, and structures	Periods of geological time, forms of business ownership Major natural resources Theory of evolution, structure of Congress

C. Procedural Knowledge: How to do something; methods of inquiry; and criteria for using skills, algorithms, techniques, and methods. Example verbs: *apply, demonstrate, illustrate, utilize*	

C1. Knowledge of subject-specific skills and algorithms
 	
C2. Knowledge of subject-specific techniques and methods
C3. Knowledge of criteria for determining when to use appropriate
    procedures
	Skills used in painting with watercolors, whole-number division
	    algorithm
	Interviewing techniques, scientific method
	Criteria used to determine when to apply a procedure involving
	    Newton's second law, criteria used to judge the feasibility of
	    using a particular method to estimate business costs

D. Metacognitive Knowledge: Knowledge of cognition in general as well as awareness and knowledge of one's own cognition. Example verbs: *judge, critique, validate*	

D1. Strategic knowledge
 	
D2. Knowledge about cognitive tasks, including appropriate contextual
    and conditional knowledge
D3. Self-knowledge
	Knowledge of outlining as a means of capturing the structure of a unit
	    of subject matter in a textbook, knowledge of the use of heuristics
	Knowledge of the types of tests particular teachers administer,
	    knowledge of the cognitive demands of different tasks
	Awareness of one's own knowledge level

Cognitive Process Dimension	
1. Remember: Retrieve relevant knowledge from long-term memory. Example verbs: *recognize, identify, recall, retrieve*	
1A. Locate knowledge in long-term memory that is consistent with presented material. 1B. Retrieve relevant knowledge from long-term memory.	Recognize the dates of important events in U.S. history. Recall the names of important people in psychology.

2. Understand: Construct meaning from instructional messages, including oral, written, and graphic communication.
    Example verbs: *interpret, clarify, paraphrase, represent, translate, exemplify, illustrate, instantiate, classify, categorize, subsume, summarize,
    abstract, generalize, compare, contrast, map, match, explain, construct, model*	

2A. Change one form of representation to another. 2B. Find a specific example or illustration of a concept or principle. 2C. Determine that something belongs to a category. 2D. Abstract a general theme or major point(s). 2E. Draw a logical conclusion from presented information. 2F. Detect correspondences between two ideas, objects, etc. 2G. Construct a cause-and-effect model of a system.	Translate from musical to verbal; paraphrase an important speech or a document. Give examples of various artistic painting styles. Classify observed or described cases of mental disorders by concept. Write a short summary of the events portrayed on a videotape. Learn a foreign language; infer grammatical principles from examples. Compare historical events to contemporary situations. Explain the causes of important eighteenth-century events in France.

Cognitive Process Dimension	
3. Apply: Carry out or use a procedure in a given situation. Example verbs: *execute, carry out, implement, use*	
3A. Apply a procedure to a familiar task. 3B. Apply a procedure to an unfamiliar task.	Divide one whole number by another whole number, both with multiple digits. Use Newton's Second Law in appropriate situations.
4. Analyze: Break material into its constituent parts and determine how the parts relate to one another and to an overall structure or purpose. Example verbs: *differentiate, discriminate, distinguish, focus, select, organize, find coherence, integrate, outline, parse, structure, attribute, deconstruct*	
4A. Distinguish relevant from irrelevant parts or important from unimportant parts of presented material. 4B. Determine how elements fit or function within a structure. 4C. Determine a point of view, bias, values, or intent underlying presented material.	Distinguish between relevant and irrelevant numbers in a mathematical word problem. Structure evidence in a historical description into evidence for and against a particular historical explanation. Determine the point of view of the author of an essay in terms of his or her perspective.
5. Evaluate: Make judgments based on criteria and standards. Example verbs: *check, coordinate, detect, monitor, test, critique, judge*	
5A. Detect inconsistencies or fallacies within a process or product; determine whether a process or product has internal consistency; detect the effectiveness of a procedure as it is being implemented. 5B. Detect inconsistencies between a product and external criteria; determine whether a product has external consistency; detect the appropriateness of a procedure for a given problem.	Determine whether a scientist's conclusions follow from observed data. Judge which of two methods is the better way to solve a given problem.
6. Create: Put elements together to form a coherent, functional whole; reorganize elements into a new pattern or structure. Example verbs: *generate, hypothesize, plan, design, produce, construct*	
6A. Come up with alternate hypotheses based on criteria. 6B. Devise a procedure for accomplishing some task. 6C. Invent a product.	Generate hypotheses to account for an observed phenomenon. Plan a research paper on a given historical topic. Build habitats for a specific purpose.

Figure 12.2   Descriptions of Revised Bloom's Cognitive Taxonomy

Note. Adapted from *A Taxonomy for Learning, Teaching, and Assessing: A Revision of Bloom's Taxonomy of Educational Objectives* by L. W. Anderson and D. R. Krathwohl, 2001, New York. Copyright 2001 by Addison Wesley Longman. Used by permission.

Figure 12.1 is a chart of the revised Cognitive Taxonomy. Each segment (or cell) represents a single developmental level, combining one step on the Cognitive Process Dimension axis with a step on the Knowledge Dimension axis. For instance, segment 2B represents Understanding (Cognitive Process Dimension) at the Conceptual Knowledge (Knowledge Dimension) level. Based on the descriptions in Figure 12.2, segment 2B would include constructing meaning from information dealing with the interrelationships among basic elements. The segments are important because each individual teaching goal must have learning objectives, learning experiences, and evaluation plans at the same developmental level. This is to ensure that the learning experiences are designed to provide exposure, practice, and feedback for students at the levels at which they will be assessed.

The practical value of the Bloom taxonomies is in the verbs that are attached to each level of each domain because they tie directly to the construction of appropriate student learning objectives. Whatever you decide is the correct order of development for your students, you can design your student learning objectives

1. Receive	
Example verbs: *ask, listen, focus, attend, take part, discuss, acknowledge, hear, be open to, retain, follow, concentrate, read, do, feel*	
Open to experience; willing to hear	Listen to instructor, take interest in class, take notes, turn up, make time for class activities, participate passively

2. Respond	
Example verbs: *react, respond, seek clarification, interpret, clarify, provide additional examples, contribute, question, help team, perform, write*	
React and participate actively	Participate actively in group, active participation in class, interest in outcomes, enthusiasm for action, probe ideas, suggest interpretation

3. Value	
Example verbs: *argue, challenge, debate, refute, confront, justify, persuade, criticize*	
Attach values and express personal opinions	Argue, challenge, debate, refute, confront, justify, persuade, criticize

4. Conceptualize Values	
Example verbs: *build, develop, formulate, defend, modify, relate, prioritize, reconcile, contrast, arrange, compare*	
Reconcile internal conflicts; develop value system	Qualify and quantify personal views, state personal position and reasons, state beliefs

5. Internalize Values	
Example verbs: *act, display, influence, solve, practice*	
Adopt belief system and philosophy	Self-reliant, behave consistently with personal values

Figure 12.3   Stages of Affective Development of College Students

From *Taxonomy of Educational Objectives: The Classification of Educational Goals. Handbook II: Affective Domain,* by D. R. Krathwohl, B. S. Bloom, and B. B. Masia, 1964. New York: McKay. Copyright 1964 by McKay. Adapted with permission.

in a consistent order, demonstrating the path of learning. In addition, you can design learning experiences appropriate to the level of development. By placing the learning objectives in order of how you think they will develop, you will have organized the progression of your learning experiences.

AFFECTIVE TAXONOMY

In 1964, Krathwohl, Bloom, and Masia published the *Taxonomy of Educational Objectives: The Classification of Educational Goals. Handbook II, The Affective Domain.* The affective taxonomy (see Figure 12.3) covers devel-

opment from being open to new experiences through the internalization of a personal value system. Emotion is linked directly to memory, which is why people remember everything about where they were when they had an emotional experience, such as hearing about an assassination. We need our students to develop their affective abilities so that they can value themselves, others, and evidence. High-level affective traits are necessary for students to be able to participate in critical-thinking discussions because conceptualizing and internalizing values are essential for Perry's (1968/1970) Commitment stage and Belenky, Clinchy, Goldberger, and Tarule's (1986) Constructed Knowing.

1. Initiation	
Example verbs: *copy, follow, replicate, repeat, adhere*	
Copy action of another; observe and replicate	Watch and repeat instructor actions

2. Manipulation	
Example verbs: *re-create, build, perform, execute, implement*	
Reproduce activity from instruction or memory	Carry out task from written or verbal instructions

3. Precision	
Example verbs: *demonstrate, complete, show, perfect, calibrate, control*	
Execute skill reliably, independent of help	Perform task or activity with expertise and to high quality without assistance or instruction

4. Articulation	
Example verbs: *construct, solve, combine, coordinate, integrate, adapt, develop, formulate, modify, master*	
Adapt and integrate expertise to satisfy a new objective	Combine activities to develop new, adaptive methods

5. Naturalization	
Example verbs: *design, specify, manage, invent*	
Automated action at a high level	Define goal and strategy to meet a strategic purpose

Figure 12.4   Psychomotor Taxonomy

Note. From "Psychomotor Taxonomy," by R. H. Dave, in *Developing and Writing Behavioral Objectives,* R. J. Armstrong (Ed.), 1970, Tucson, AZ: Educational Innovators Press. Adapted with permission.

PSYCHOMOTOR TAXONOMY

Bloom was not involved in the development of a taxonomy for the psychomotor domain, but it is still included as part of the Bloom Taxonomies. Dave (1970), Harrow (1972), and Simpson (1972) each published a psychomotor taxonomy. The Simpson and Harrow psychomotor taxonomies are directed more toward the development of children. The version by Dave (Figure 12.4) is the most applicable to higher education, because it can apply to modern business and social skills, as well as the originally imagined physical abilities. The stages of the Dave psychomotor taxonomy are initiation, manipulation, precision, articulation, and naturalization. These relate to the developmental steps Gardner (1993) identified in the bodily-kinesthetic domain, as well as adaptation to new experiences that require combining activities to develop new methods.

PATHWAYS THROUGH THE TAXONOMIES

The designers of the taxonomies contend that everyone goes through each step on the way to the next one, in the order they have specified. From Kolb we know that different people like to enter the cycle of learning at different points. As a result, I have created two different developmental models of Bloom's cognitive taxonomy. One is for reflectors (reflective observation, or RO) and theorists (abstract conceptualization, or AC), who follow the originally described path from "remember" to "understand" (Figure 12.5), but this model shows application as a back-and-forth step as learners try out their ideas. The other developmental model is for activists (active experimentation, or AE) and pragmatists (concrete experience, or CE), who jump right from "remember" to "apply" and get to "understand" later (Figure 12.6).

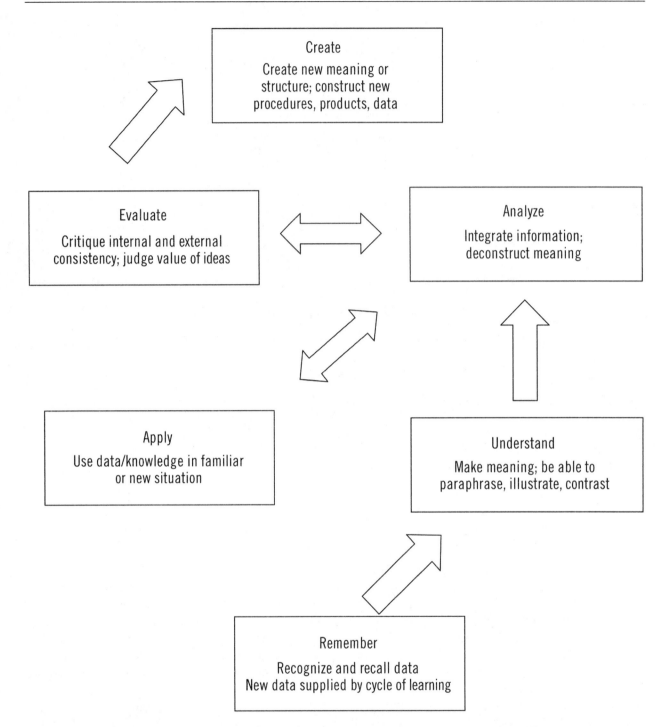

Figure 12.5   Developmental Pathways of Revised Bloom Cognitive Taxonomy for Kolb Reflectors (RO) and Theorists (AC)

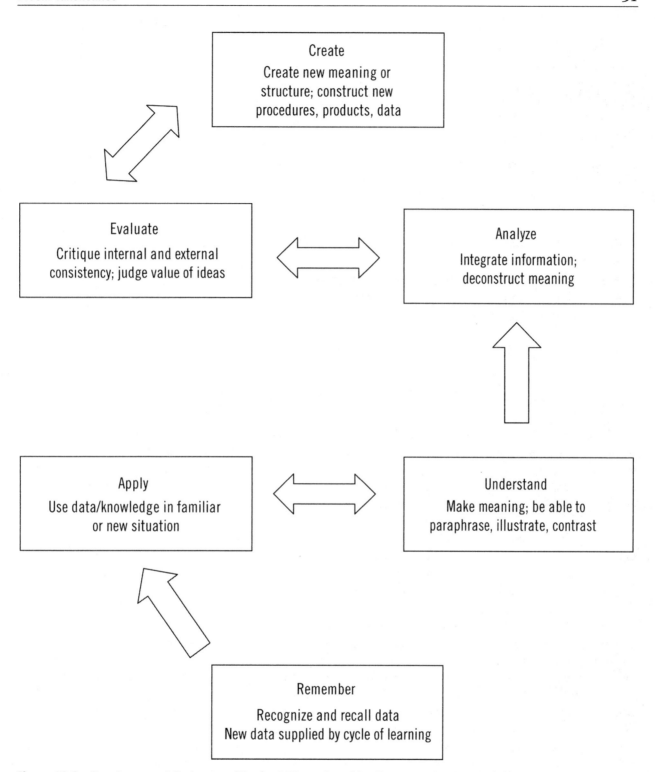

Figure 12.6   Developmental Pathways of Revised Bloom Cognitive Taxonomy for Kolb Activists (AE) and Pragmatists (CE)

CHAPTER 13

Motivation

LEARNING OBJECTIVES

Readers of this chapter will be able to:

- Describe extrinsic and intrinsic motivations for learning.
- Explain how extrinsic motivators can decrease motivation to learn.
- Describe two elements that influence a learner's motivation.
- Describe a "natural learning environment."

EXTRINSIC MOTIVATION IS ENCOURAGEMENT FROM AN outside force; behavior is performed based on the expectation of an outside reward, such as money or grades. Extrinsic rewards can be abused to bribe or coerce people into doing something that they would not do on their own. These rewards are contingent on the satisfactory completion of a task. The problems with extrinsic motivators are numerous. For instance, extrinsic rewards do not produce permanent changes, they reduce interest and motivation, and they often are felt as controlling.

When a classroom is run on natural, intrinsic motivation, emphasis is on learning and being part of the environment, not on rewards. To create a learning environment in which students' needs are addressed, instructors must understand their students' interests, beliefs, and concerns: in short, their motivations. Four factors are essential to meeting motivational needs: promoting success, arousing curiosity, allowing originality, and encouraging relationships. Success can be developed by clearly defining what success is, valuing it in the classroom, and helping students see how they can attain it. Authentic issues awaken curiosity. Curiosity can be aroused by making sure that lessons offer fragmented or contradictory information, which puts students in the active role of solving the unknown.

Originality can be promoted by allowing many opportunities for students to express autonomy. Finally, by encouraging relationships, students' innate need for interpersonal involvement is fostered. When factors such as these are included in a classroom, students are naturally involved and driven to learn because their intrinsic motivation is heightened.

Based on the review of the research on motivation, Bain (2004) states that "performance—not just motivation—can decrease when subjects believe that other people are trying to control them. If students study only because they want to get a good grade or be the best in the class, they do not achieve as much as they do when they learn because they are interested. . . . Most extrinsic motivators decrease motivation" (p. 33).

The American Psychological Association and Mid-Continent Regional Education Laboratory developed 14 learner-centered principles that address three categories: cognitive and metacognitive factors; motivational and affective factors; and developmental, personal, social, and individual difference factors (see section 5; Alexander & Murphy, 1998). According to Salisbury-Glennon, Young, and Stefanou (2001), the APA learner-centered principles "are based on a synthesis of a large body of research . . .

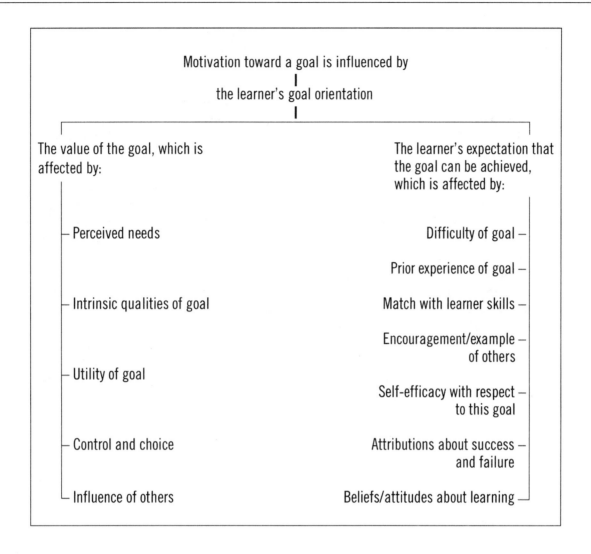

Motivation toward a goal is influenced by
|
the learner's goal orientation
|

The value of the goal, which is affected by:

— Perceived needs

— Intrinsic qualities of goal

— Utility of goal

— Control and choice

— Influence of others

The learner's expectation that the goal can be achieved, which is affected by:

Difficulty of goal —

Prior experience of goal —

Match with learner skills —

Encouragement/example — of others

Self-efficacy with respect — to this goal

Attributions about success — and failure

Beliefs/attitudes about learning —

Figure 13.1 An Amalgamated Model of Motivation

Note. From *Learning and Motivation in the Postsecondary Classroom* (p. 146), by M. Svinicki, 2004, Bolton, MA: Anker. Copyright 2004 by Anker. Reprinted with permission.

that learners learn best when they are intrinsically motivated, self-efficacious, and pursue learning-focused or master goals" (p. 24).

The exceptional teachers in Bain's (2004) study "avoided using grades to persuade students to study. . . . [Rather they] invoked the subject, the questions it raises, and the promises it makes to any learner" (p. 36). According to Svinicki (2004), when students are asked about their best teachers, "motivation is almost always the number one quality listed" (p. 141). Figure 13.1 presents an "Amalgamated Model of Motivation" developed by Svinicki. In the model, she shows how two overriding elements influence the learner's motivation:

the value of the goal and the expectation that the goal can be achieved (p. 146).

VALUE OF THE GOAL

What importance does the learner place on reaching a goal? For instance, how will the course "give them an edge in the world of work" (Svinicki, 2004, p. 148). How interesting, novel, or challenging is the goal itself? How useful is the goal in the short and long term? How much control does the student have over reaching the goal? How valuable is the goal to other people?

All of these factors go into the value a student places on a goal. Increasing the *value* of a goal to students is, according to Svinicki, the easier part of motivation.

EXPECTATION THAT THE GOAL CAN BE ACHIEVED

Students may believe, or think, they can or cannot achieve a particular goal. Do they think they have the ability? How difficult do they perceive the goal to be? What has their prior experience told them? How do they understand how their prior abilities will help them meet new challenges? What are the students' beliefs about the nature of ability and their self-confidence as learners? To persist, students need to find the goal both challenging and attainable.

The exceptional teachers in Bain's (2004) study focused on creating "a natural learning environment" to motivate their students (2004, p. 99). They believe that

> people tend to learn most effectively (in ways that make a sustained, substantial, and positive influence on the way they act, think, or feel) when (1) they are trying to solve problems (intellectual, physical, artistic, practical, or abstract) that they find intriguing, beautiful, or important; (2) they are able to do so in a challenging yet supportive environment in which they can feel a sense of control over their own education; (3) they can work collaboratively with other learners to grapple with the problems; (4) they believe that their work will be considered fairly and honestly; and (5) if they can try, fail, and receive feedback from expert learners in advance of and separate from any judgment of their efforts. (p. 109)

Finally, the teachers in Bain's study achieved their success at creating deep and sustained learning by designing courses to "avoid extrinsic motivators and to foster intrinsic ones, moving students toward learning goals and a mastery orientation. They gave students as much control over their own education as possible and displayed both a strong interest in their learning and a faith in their abilities" (p. 35).

CHAPTER 14

Metaphors for the Teaching><Learning Connection

LEARNING OBJECTIVES

Readers of this chapter will be able to:

- Describe metaphors instructors and students use to describe teaching and learning.
- Describe their own teaching><learning metaphor.
- Describe the developmental levels of teaching.

BECAUSE WE CANNOT SEE DIRECTLY THE MENTAL models we each have for teaching and learning, by using metaphors, such as analogies, similes, and visual models, we can make explicit how we (and our students) understand the teaching><learning connection. Howard Pollio (1986) collected examples of how 800 faculty members and graduate students visualized the teaching and learning process. From thematic analysis, he identified three metaphors that accounted for the majority of responses:

1. Containers: Knowledge is a substance held by teachers and poured into students.
2. Journey-Guide: The teacher takes the students on a journey to find knowledge.
3. Master-Disciple: Knowledge is a skill or habit students learn to do by imitating and never questioning the master.

From more than 700 faculty members in his many workshops on teaching, Grasha (1996) identified a longer list of metaphors, including layer-coach, mata-dor, bartender, attorney before a jury, director of a play, lion tamer, gardener, midwife, evangelist, and choreographer (p. 36). Grasha also surveyed his students for *their* metaphors of teaching and learning. As

you would expect, the students had a different perspective on many of the faculty metaphors. For instance, whereas teachers used the container metaphor of feeding knowledge to students, two of Grasha's students "described what they received from teachers as 'junk food' and as 'bad tasting medicine that you don't want to take but deep down inside you know it's good for you'" (p. 35). When teachers used the journey-guide metaphor, one of the students "noted that the teachers were guiding them on a 'great interplanetary adventure,' and another felt 'lost in space'" (p. 35). Fewer than 2% of Grasha's 1,500 student-generated metaphors describe teaching as master-disciple. He says, "Perhaps it relates to their stage of development, but undergraduates do not view themselves as disciples to great masters" (p. 35).

In 1986, an amazing group of higher-education scholars who were authors of current reports on the state of higher education met at Wingspread, a conference center in Racine, Wisconsin, to generate a statement of principles to guide undergraduate education. The list of seven principles appeared in the *AAHE Bulletin* (Chickering & Gamson, 1987) and as a stand-alone booklet. Several hundred thousand copies of the booklet were requested and distributed by the Johnson Foundation, and many more copies have been printed

Areas of Concern	Pre-stage	Stage 1	Stage 2	Stage 3
Relationship to Students	I'm not really a teacher, OR, I will be a perfect teacher.	Can I do it right? Am I good enough to pull it off?	I'm orchestrating student learning.	Teaching is a partnership with the students, both individually and as a group.
Content and Course Planning	Imposed from outside.	Content is primary, most important thing.	Students' grasp of content, motivation of students.	Content is secondary, meta concerns: seeing beyond the requirements, taking a more critical eye toward evaluative content.
Students	Idealized or unknown.	Irrelevant, the opposition.	Performing animals, reflection of instructor.	Partners, of primary importance.
Evaluation and Monitoring Progress	Don't think about it.	Clueless.	I have to fix it. Why do my students rate my teaching this way?	Selectivity, discrimination, ability to perceive what does or doesn't come from oneself.
Methods of Teaching	Alternatives exist?	Basic competency, learn to deal with.	Reevaluate teaching, cause certain effects on students, learning students, learning to do it.	Choosing among methods, expertise.

Figure 14.1   Developmental Levels of Teaching

Note. From "Combining Departmental Training with Central Support: A Research Project," by M. Svinicki, T. Sullivan, M. Greer, and M. Diaz, 1991, presented at Third National Conference on the Training and Employment of Graduate Teaching Assistants, Austin, TX. Adapted with permission.

by colleges and universities. The Seven Principles (see section 5 for a full description) state that good practices encourage student-faculty contact, cooperation among students, active learning, prompt feedback, time on task, and high expectations; and respect diverse talents and ways of learning. The principles correlate directly with what we have found about how students learn and can be used equally for graduate as for undergraduate courses. Each principle is backed up by what Mary Deane Sorcinelli (1991) refers to as "five decades of teaching and learning in higher education" (p. 13). Sorcinelli reports that "the Seven Principles for Good Practice in Undergraduate Education provide substantive research-based advice that can enrich our understanding and practice of teaching and learning at the college level. Results of research on student-faculty contact, prompt feedback, and active involvement in learning are especially encouraging" (pp. 22–23).

Based on good practice, we can divide metaphors into those that are useful for encouraging student learn-

ing and those that are not. For instance, the Player-Coach metaphor, which reflects the vision of a sports team, invokes all of the Seven Principles for Good Practice: student-faculty contact, cooperation among students (team members), active learning, prompt feedback, time on task, high expectations, and diverse talents. On the other hand, the metaphors of Lion Tamer and Matador may provide prompt feedback (the whip and sword) and even time on task, but the other of the principles would not be honored. As professors develop and learn more about themselves and their students, metaphors for teaching and learning change from less useful to more useful for encouraging learning.

Obviously, one of the most pressing issues in the development of college instructors is how to shift their focus from their own survival issues to an understanding of student learning. Shirley Ronkowski (1993) identified nine concerns of teaching assistants, which she divided into three stages: basic survival, skill improvement, and student learning. Svinicki, Sullivan, Greer, and Diaz (1991) created a prototype developmental scheme based on instructors' concerns about teaching (Figure 14.1) that includes three stages and a prestage. They found that as instructors develop they move from survival skills (including ignoring entire responsibilities), to "orchestration" of student learning and, finally, in the best cases, to "partnership" with their students.

My graduate students draw their metaphors for teaching and learning at the beginning and the end of the year of their "Preparing Future Faculty Program."

Figure 14.2 (pp. 58–59) shows some of their changing metaphors over time. Two students drew beginning metaphors showing teachers pouring content into containers; these changed, after a year of research on teaching and learning, to teachers watering a blooming tree and a group of students. Another student drew a professor sending concepts via a watering can to student brains displayed on desks; after a year she drew a circle of learners that includes the teacher. A fourth student's beginning metaphor was the sun shining on flowers and trees; at the end of the year her metaphor for teaching and learning was managing a baseball team.

Two Examples of Changes from

Pouring Knowledge into Students   **to**   **Providing Rain for Student Growth**

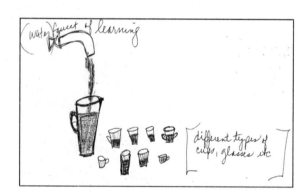

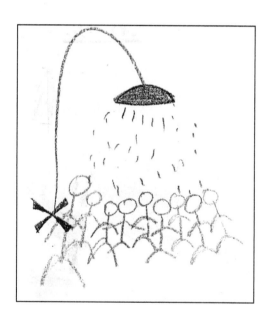

Change from Watering Brains to Forming a Circle of Students and Teacher

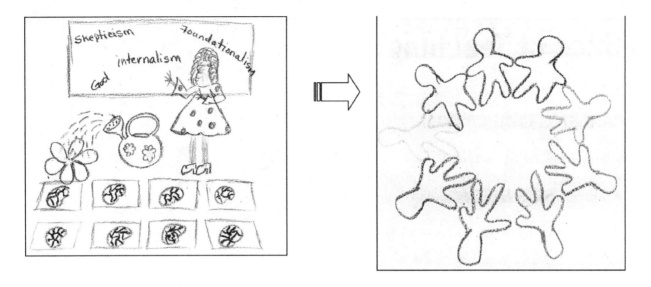

Change from Providing Sun for Plants to Managing a Baseball Team

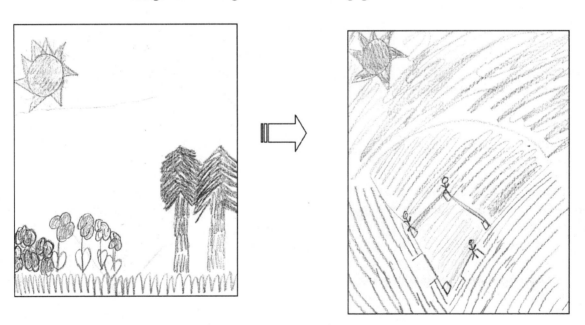

Figure 14.2   Metaphors for Teaching

CHAPTER 15

Ethics of Teaching

LEARNING OBJECTIVES

Readers of this chapter will be able to:
- State nine ethical principles of college teachers.
- Describe the essential responsibilities inherent in each principle.

COLLEGE AND UNIVERSITY "PROFESSING" IS A VERY IN-fluential profession, but there are almost no requirements for entry to the field except the willingness of an institution to hire someone. In response to the need for professional standards, the Society for Teaching and Learning in Higher Education (STLHE) developed *Ethical Principles in University Teaching* for consideration and adaptation by Canadian colleges and universities (see section 5 for the full document). STLHE (1996) "believes that implementation of an ethical code similar to that described . . . will be advantageous to university teachers (e.g., in removing ambiguity concerning teaching responsibilities); and will contribute significantly to improvement of teaching" (preamble). According to the ethical principles, college teachers should have content competence, pedagogical competence, be able to deal with "sensitive topics," understand and contribute to student development, avoid inappropriate relationships with students, maintain confidentiality, provide valid assessment of students, and have respect for their colleagues and the institutions at which they teach.

Content competence requires that instructors stay up to date on course material, including prerequisites, even if it is not of particular interest to them, and that they present material reflecting any differences of opin-ion and perspectives. It also requires that what is taught include all content stated in the course objectives. The result of failing to adhere to this principle includes not being current in the field, teaching only what is of interest to the instructor, and misinterpreting evidence in order to support a personal theory.

Pedagogical competence requires that instructors design their courses to tie together the learning objectives, learning experiences, and assessment strategies. It also requires that instructors stay current on research into pedagogical strategies and provide their students opportunities to practice and receive feedback on their efforts before they are graded. This ethical principle means that the level of testing must match the level of objectives and experiences, which sometimes is disparaged as "teaching to the test." Yet, it would be unethical to test what has *not* been taught.

Ethically dealing with sensitive topics requires that the instructor be able to discuss issues in an open and honest way. To do this, it is important that the instructor acknowledge to students the difficulties and complexities of the subject, allow each person's point of view to be stated, and provide a safe classroom environment for frank discussion. Failure to adhere to this principle results in what students perceive as a closed environment, in which they will either withdraw from interaction with the issues or rebel against the instructor's or text's interpretation.

It is the responsibility of instructors to facilitate students' development and avoid exploitation or discrimination. This includes treating students with respect and not exploiting the power difference between teachers and students. Having students do research on the instructor's behalf not related to course goals or taking sole intellectual credit for student collaboration represents failure to adhere to the ethical principle of fostering student development.

By not entering into dual relationships with students, ethical instructors avoid actual and perceived favoritism toward particular students. This includes, of course, romantic relationships and those involving family members, lending money to or borrowing it from students, accepting or giving gifts, and excessive socializing.

Ethical instructors maintain confidentiality of student grades and private communications unless they receive authorization from students to release the information. Violations of this principle include posting identifiable student grades, leaving graded papers where others could see them, and providing information to employers. In the United States there are strict laws governing what information can be released under what circumstances.

It is not ethical to grade students on material or skills that are not included in the course learning objectives or that students did not have opportunities to practice. Ethical instructors conduct valid assessment of students. Their grading processes are open and fair.

Finally, ethical instructors display respect for their colleagues and institutions. This includes not making disparaging remarks about administrators, other professors, or university policies. Good practice also includes referring students to courses in other departments or with other professors, and implementing institutional policies on assessment and academic honesty.

CHAPTER 16

Designing Learning Experiences

LEARNING OBJECTIVES

Readers of this chapter will be able to:

- Clearly state across-the-curriculum learning experiences that may be incorporated into their courses.
- Describe learning experiences representing each of the four clusters of Grasha teaching and learning styles.
- Place learning experiences into Blueprint segments with their teaching goals and learning objectives.

WE KNOW FROM THE WORK OF ZULL, BLOOM, AND Kolb that learning is a physical change in synaptic pathways in the brain brought about by confronting real-life situations that either confirm or challenge our mental models. David and Roger Johnson and Karl Smith (1998), longtime scholars of active learning, view teaching in terms of several principal constructs:

- knowledge is discovered, transformed, and extended by students;
- students actively construct their own knowledge;
- learning is a social enterprise in which students need to interact with the instructor and classmates;
- faculty effort should be aimed at developing students' competencies and talents;
- education is a personal transaction among students and between faculty and students as they work together;
- learning is best when it takes place within a cooperative context; and
- teaching is a complex application of theory and research that requires considerable instructor training and continuous refinement of skills and procedures. (1:9–1:12)

Charles Bonwell and James Eison (1991) describe a continuum of possible classroom actions that increase in students' activity. The passive end of the continuum would include such things as sitting in class inattentively, dividing one's concentration between episodes of daydreaming and periods of attentiveness to the lecture, and listening and occasionally taking literal notes. . . . Students' involvement can be . . . increased by the instructor's use of strategies such as discussion-leading and questioning techniques skillfully to engage students in a personal exploration of the subject matter . . . and using presentations, debates, and role-playing activities by students. (p. 2)

For each type of learning experience (LE) an instructor decides to use, it is essential that it fall into the same category of the Bloom Taxonomy as the teaching goals (TGs) and learning objectives (LOs), so that students can practice the skills and knowledge that will be required in the evaluation plan (EP). The blueprint segment in Figure 16.1 shows examples of two levels of TGs, LOs, and LEs for an introductory psychology course.

Cognitive Design Blueprint

TG = Teaching Goal   LO = Learning Objective   LE = Learning Experience   EP = Evaluation Plan

Introductory Psychology Course

SEGMENT
Knowledge Dimension: Factual Knowledge
Cognitive Process: Remember

TG	Students will learn the facts and concepts of twentieth-century psychology.
LO	Students completing this course will be able to list the five most influential psychologists of the twentieth century.
LE	Students will read text and listen to lecture.
EP	

SEGMENT
Knowledge Dimension: Conceptual Knowledge
Cognitive Process: Apply

TG	Students will understand how the psychological theories of the twentieth century apply to current personal problems.
LO	Students completing this course will be able to apply concepts of twentieth-century psychology to current personal problems.
LE	Students will complete an internship at a local community mental health center.
EP	

As the course develops, the blueprint will include an evaluation plan (EP) to assess the students' learning.

Figure 16.1   Example Segments of a Course Design Blueprint

ACROSS-THE-CURRICULUM LEARNING EXPERIENCES

Whatever the content or course level, there are certain learning experiences that are essential life skills for living in the twenty-first century and should be developed in every course: active learning, reading, writing, information literacy, quantitative literacy, critical thinking, and transdisciplinarity. Some of these may be required to meet particular institutional or departmental goals.

Active Learning

Bonwell and Eison (1991) provide a working definition of active learning as "anything that involves students in doing things and thinking about the things they are doing" (p. 2). They describe characteristics of active learning, compared to traditional lecture-based courses, as follows:

- Students are involved in more than listening.
- Less emphasis is placed on transmitting information and more on developing students' skills.
- Students are involved in higher-order thinking (analysis, synthesis, evaluation).
- Students are engaged in activities (e.g., reading, discussing, writing).
- Greater emphasis is placed on students' exploration of their own attitudes and values. (p. 2)

Dee Fink (2003) divides "active" learning into two components: experiences and reflection (see Figure

Passive and Active Learning

Figure 16.2   Tasks Involved in Passive and Active Learning

Note. From *Creating Significant Learning Experience: An Integrated Approach to Designing College Courses* (p. 104) by L. D. Fink, 2003, San Francisco: Jossey-Bass. Copyright 2005 by Jossey-Bass. Used by permission.

16.2). He believes that students need to "actually do that which we want them to learn to do" (p. 105). In addition, he reminds us that "reflection, the second major component of active learning, was part of the original definition, but Bonwell and Eison did not develop it as fully as their experiential component" (p. 105). Fink says that because

> people are meaning-making beings. . . . We make meaning based on our experiences and on the information and ideas we encounter. However, this is where a potential problem crops up. Whenever someone has a new experience or encounters a new idea, those events automatically have an initial meaning. But this initial meaning may remain buried at the unconscious or subconscious level. When this happens, the meaning may be limited, distorted, or even destructive. As humans, we have the capacity to change the meaning of our ideas and experiences—but only when we pull our original meaning up to the conscious level and reflect on what new meaning we want those ideas or experiences to have. Only then do we become *meaning-making* beings, rather than simply meaning-receiving beings. (p. 111)

Fink proposes three ways that active learning can be incorporated effectively into a course:

Strategy #1: Create rich learning experiences in which students are able to simultaneously achieve multiple kinds of significant learning. Some sug-

gestions are debates, role-playing, service learning, and other authentic projects.

Strategy #2: Find new ways to introduce students to information and ideas. Use methods such as those Barbara Walvoord (2004) uses to have the first student exposure to new material *outside* of precious class time. Walvoord divides learning opportunities into three types: "Students with Teacher (Class)," "Student 'Study' Time," and "Teacher Alone." Figure 30 [Figure 16.3] shows Walvoord's interactive method in which students first learn about material through reading, videos, or other media, and class time is used to respond to and process the material.

Strategy #3: Promote in-depth writing on the learning process. Have students write for themselves, using journaling and learning portfolios, and for others, including teachers, other students, and people outside the class. Activities should include "substantive writing," about the subject of the course, and "reflective writing," about "What am I learning? Of what value is this? How did I learn best, most comfortably, with difficulty? What else do I need to learn?" (p. 116).

Reading across the Curriculum

Most of us learn to read in the early grades and then move from "learning to read" to "reading to learn" around the third grade. Although there are "developmental" programs for struggling college students, there

	Students With Teacher (Class)	Student "Study" Time	Teacher Alone
Traditional Lecture Method	First exposure to new material	Process material	Respond to student work
Inter-Active Method	Process response	First exposure to new material	

Figure 16.3   Use Class Time for Process and Response

Note. From *Teaching Well, Saving Time: Two Powerful Principles,* by B. E. Walvoord, 2004, keynote presentation at the national Lilly Conference on College Teaching at Miami University, Oxford, Ohio. Reprinted from handout with permission.

are few programs on how to move to college-level reading for other students. Yet "language literacy, the ability to use language effectively, determines how successful individuals can be in many facets of life. Reading is a critical aspect of language literacy" (Cole, 1997, p. 1).

As you design your course, unless you have direct proof otherwise, you should not expect that students in your course are able to read at a critical level or can read the type of texts in your discipline.

College reading programs offer courses and tutoring

Techniques for Skillful Reading

Ways of Reading
. . . it is crucial for college students to develop reading strategies and techniques which will aid in learning, understanding, and retaining key concepts from textbooks, essays, novels, technical materials, and other kinds of reading . . .

Visualizing
". . . can help to improve your critical comprehension of a text . . . will enhance the other reading strategies . . . also your understanding of the way the pieces of an essay/novel/story work together and allows you to make connection between a number of texts."

Reading With and Against the Grain
"a good reader is one who reads actively, interacting with the text in many ways . . . thinking about and considering what a writer does not say as well as what she does say are all parts of critical thinking and reading . . . reading 'with and against the grain' enables you to fully engage with a text and an author's ideas moving toward developing your own reading."

Four Reading Rates
"to maximize your comprehension of a text, adjust your reading style, technique, and rate to accommodate the type of text your [sic] are reading . . ."

Recognizing Signal Words
"Transitions or signal words help you, the reader, follow the directions of a writer's thought . . . Common signal words show emphasis, addition, comparison or contrast, illustration, and cause and effect."

Figure 16.4 Techniques to Help Students Develop the Abilities Necessary to Deal with Advanced Texts

Note. From California State Polytechnic University, Pomona, www.csupomona.edu/~lrc/crsp/techniques.html.

at a "nonbaccalaureate" level, in that if there is credit for a course it does not count toward the degree. One of the most comprehensive programs is the College Reading Skills Program (CRSP) at the California State Polytechnic University, Pomona. Figure 16.4 shows the "Techniques for Skillful Reading" as they are described in the CRSP online program description. Basically, reading is an active learning experience tied directly to critical thinking and can be taught across disciplines.

Writing across the Curriculum

Bruce Speck (2002), an expert in designing and grading writing assignments, says:

> When I talk about competence in teaching writing, I have in mind all faculty, not just those faculty who have particular credentials in teaching writing. Although colleges and universities hire professors with a specialization in writing to teach courses such as freshmen composition, advanced composition, business writing, technical writing, creative writing, and so on, the teaching of writing is the responsibility of the entire faculty. Why? Because writing is not like other subjects. . . . Writing, just like speaking, applies to all the content areas. (p. 7)

Speck (2002) goes on to say:

> A professor of composition does not need to know anything about nuclear physics to teach writing, but a professor of nuclear physics needs to know about writing pedagogy to teach students how to write in the physics class. In fact, the professor of composition, in virtually all cases, cannot provide adequate insight for students to produce acceptable writing in nuclear physics, particularly when writing assignments call on students to use the form, language, and style unique to scientific writing in general and the writing of physics in particular. (p. 7)

Because you are a scholar of the texts of your discipline, you also are an expert in how to write in your discipline. You grade your students' writing, which means you have developed (possibly implicit) criteria for acceptable composition. Teaching writing actually is teaching students about editing and rewriting. It does no good to provide feedback to students if they do not have a chance to use your feedback to improve

their efforts. It is much more useful to assign a few moderately sized writing assignments with a process and time for feedback and rewriting than a larger number of small assignments or one big research project without the opportunity for rewriting. LeBlanc (1988) suggests that revision is not just one step in the writing process. He states that revision "is located in the whole of the writing process—from point of inscription to final draft" (p. 34).

Speck (2002) is in favor of collaborative writing because "texts depend on other texts" (p. 5). "Clearly," he says, "writing is inherently collaborative—whether academic or 'creative'—and the interreliance of a text on other texts, the intertextuality of texts, is one major piece of evidence that supports the inherent collaborative nature of writing" (p. 6). Instructors frequently assign group reports without realizing that they are using a cooperative learning technique, defined as "the instructional use of small groups so that students work together to maximize their own and each other's learning" (Johnson, Johnson, & Smith, 1998, p. 12). Speck (2002) writes, "Collaborative writing fits nicely with the premises that support cooperative learning and logically shares the pedagogical presuppositions of active learning" (p. 8).

The first, and possibly most difficult, task is creating the writing assignment. Speck (2002) recommends that an assignment include the "real" purpose of the assignment (what will students learn?), the audience for the piece (teacher? peers? outside community members?), a realistic schedule (including time for students to critique peers' efforts), requirements (such as length, typestyle, headings, graphics), and grading criteria (pp. 44–45). Speck states:

> One implication of designing collaborative writing assignments so that they stimulate active learning is that the professor should conceptualize the entire writing process for any particular project before producing a writing assignment. How long will students have to complete the assignment? How many drafts are they required to produce? How will students' writing be evaluated? How does a particular writing assignment fit with the overall objectives of the course? (p. 43)

Other responsibilities of the instructor are assigning groups, teaching collaboration, managing the group process, and grading. These areas are covered later in this and the next chapter.

Information Literacy across the Curriculum

Information literacy is the ability to search for and evaluate the quality of information, particularly information found through the Internet. It is essential for college students in all fields. In 2000, the American Library Association (ALA) promulgated "Information Literacy Competency Standards for Higher Education" that promote active learning and critical thinking. The standards state that the "information literate student"

1. determines the nature and extent of the information needed
2. accesses needed information effectively and efficiently
3. evaluates information and its sources critically and incorporates selected information into his or her knowledge base and value system
4. individually, or as a member of a group, uses information effectively to accomplish a specific purpose, and
5. understands many of the economic, legal, and social issues surrounding the use of information and accesses and uses information ethically and legally. (ALA, 2000)

The Standards include performance indicators and outcomes, most of which are clearly written learning objectives. Figure 16.5 presents excerpts of the ALA standards.

Quantitative Literacy across the Curriculum

Many aspects of twenty-first-century life require as high a competency in using numbers as language. "The Case for Quantitative Literacy" (Quantitative Literacy Design Team, 2001) sets out the following argument:

The world of the twenty-first century is a world awash in numbers. Headlines use quantitative measures to report increases in gasoline prices, changes in SAT scores, risks of dying from colon cancer and numbers of refugees from the latest ethnic war. Advertisements use numbers to compete over costs of cell phone contracts and low interest car loans. Sports reporting abounds in team statistics and odds on forthcoming competitions. (p. 1)

Numeracy, mathematical literacy, and quantitative literacy are similar concepts. *Numeracy* is defined as "at homeness" with numbers and "the ability to have some appreciation and understanding of information which is presented in mathematical terms" (Cockcroft, 1982). The Organization for Economic Co-Operation and Development (OECD) Program for International Student Assessment (OECD/PISA, 2003) uses the term *mathematical literacy*, which it defines as "the capacities of students to analyze, reason, and communicate ideas effectively as they pose, formulate, solve, and interpret mathematical problems in a variety of situations" (p. 24). Lynn Steen and her colleagues on the Quantitative Literacy Design Team (QLDT) (2001) at the National Council on Education (NCE) state:

A different way to think about quantitative literacy is to look not at definitions but at actions, not at what numeracy is but how it is expressed. Many manifestations are commonplace and obviously important, yet they are not the real reason for the increasing emphasis on numeracy. These include, for example,

- Estimating how to split a lunch bill three ways.
- Comparing price options for leasing or purchasing a car.
- Reading and understanding nutrition labels.
- Scaling recipes up and down and converting units of volume and weight. (p. 7)

Including quantitative literacy across the curriculum involves the creation of what the Mathematics Council of the Alberta Teachers' Association (1996) calls "worthwhile tasks" (p. 10), another term for authentic assignments. Worthwhile tasks "require that students reason about different strategies and outcomes, weigh the pros and cons of alternatives, and pursue particular paths" (p. 10). The NCE QLDT (QLDT, 2001) describes how academic disciplines are requiring significant quantitative (as opposed to strictly mathematical) preparation:

- Biology now requires computer mathematics (for mapping genomes) . . . [and] probability (for heredity).
- The stunning impact of computer graphics in the visual arts (film, photography, sculpture) have made parts of mathematics, especially calculus, geometry, and computer algorithms, very important in a field that formerly was relatively unquantitative.

Information Literacy Competency Standards for Higher Education*

Standard One [KNOW]
The information literate student determines the nature and extent of the information needed.
    Performance Indicators:
        1.   Defines and articulates the need for information
        2.   Identifies a variety of types and formats of potential sources for information
        3.   Considers the costs and benefits of acquiring the needed information
        4.   Reevaluates the nature and extent of the information needed

Standard Two [ACCESS]
The information literate student accesses the needed information effectively and efficiently.
    Performance Indicators:
        1.   Selects the most appropriate investigative methods or information retrieval systems for accessing the needed information
        2.   Constructs and implements effectively-designed search strategies
        3.   Retrieves information online or in person using a variety of methods
        4.   Refines the search strategy as necessary
        5.   Extracts, records, and manages the information and its sources

Standard Three [EVALUATE]
The information literate student evaluates information and its sources critically and incorporates selected information into his or her knowledge base and value system.
    Performance Indicators:
        1.   Summarizes the main ideas to construct new concepts
        2.   Articulates and applies internal criteria for evaluating both the information and its sources
        3.   Synthesizes main ideas to construct new concepts
        4.   Compares new knowledge with prior knowledge to determine the value added, contradictions, or other unique characteristics of the information
        5.   Determines whether the new knowledge has an impact on the individual's value system and takes steps to reconcile the differences
        6.   Validates understanding and interpretation of the information through discourse with other individuals, subject-area experts, and/or practitioners
        7.   Determines whether the initial query should be revised

Standard Four [USE]
The information literate student, individually or as a member of a group, uses information efficiently to accomplish a specific purpose.
    Performance Indicators:
        1.   Applies new and prior information to the planning and creation of a particular product or performance
        2.   Revises the development process for the product or performance
        3.   Communicates the product or performance effectively to others

Standard Five [ETHICS]
The information literate student understands many of the economic, legal, and social issues surrounding the use of information and accesses and uses information ethically and legally.
    Performance Indicators:
        1.   Understands many of the ethical, legal, and socio-economic issues surrounding information and information technology
        2.   Follows laws, regulations, institutional policies, and etiquette related to the access and use of information resources
        3.   Acknowledges the use of information in communicating the product or performance

*The complete standards document, developed by the Association of College and Research Libraries, is available at www.ala.org/ala/acrl/acrlstandards/informationliteracycompetency.htm#stan.

Sample Framework for Integrating Information Literacy Into a Course

Standard Two
The information literate student accesses the needed information effectively and efficiently.

Performance Indicator 2: The information literate student constructs and implements effectively-designed search strategies

Learning Objectives	Course Methods	Assignment *(opportunity to practice what has been taught)*	Evaluation
Describes a general process for searching for information	Class discussions	As a first step in completing an assignment (e.g., a research paper), students develop a plan with steps for the process from start to finish	Learning Assessment (grading)
	Library workshop: Incorporating library resources and services into the research process		Method and criteria for assessing student learning
Gathers and evaluates information			
			Teaching Evaluation
Appropriately modifies the search plan as new insights are gained	Lectures	Students keep a research journal documenting how they located information	Students evaluate teacher's performance
	Tutorials		

Figure 16.5 Standards for Information Literacy Developed by the Association of College and Research Libraries

Note. From Gale Burrow and Kimberly Franklin presentation at the Claremont Graduate University, Preparing Future Faculty Professional Development Practicum "Information Literacy Across the Curriculum" 2/8/2005. Used with permission.

- Increasingly, interpretation of historical events depends on analysis of evidence provided either by numerical data (e.g., government statistics, economic indicators) or through verification and dating of artifacts.
- Even the study of language has been influenced by quantitative and logical methods, especially in linguistics, concordances, and the new field of computer translation. (p. 9)

The QLDT (2001) reports that quantitative tools are used among a wide range of professions:

- Lawyers rely on careful logic to build their cases and on subtle arguments about probability to establish or refute "reasonable doubt."
- Social workers need to understand complex state and federal regulations about income and expenses in order to explain and verify their clients' personal budgets.
- Journalists need a sophisticated understanding of quantitative issues (especially of risks, rates,

samples, surveys, and statistical evidence) in order to develop an informed and skeptical understanding of reports in the news.
- Chefs use quantitative tools to plan schedules, balance costs vs. value of ingredients, and monitor nutritional balance of meals. (p. 10)

In addition, personal health decisions include

- Interpreting medical statistics and formulating relevant questions about different options for treatment in relation to known risks and specifics of one's own condition.
- Weighing costs, benefits, and health risks of heavily advertised new drugs.
- Calibrating eating and exercise habits in relation to health. (pp. 10–11)

Managers need to use quantitative skills to "look for patterns in data to identify trends in costs, sales, and demand" or develop "a business plan, including pricing, inventory, and staffing strategy" (QLDT, 2001, p. 11).

And workers use quantitative skills to produce schedules, using work-related formulas, and maintain and use quality control charts.

The QLDT (2001) writes:

A list of skills is more comforting than a list of elements or expressions since skills are more immediately recognizable as something taught and learned in school. Moreover, many people believe that skills must precede applications and that once learned, quantitative skills can be applied whenever needed. Unfortunately, considerable evidence about the associative nature of learning suggests that this approach works very imper-

fectly. For most students, skills learned free of context are skills devoid of meaning and utility. To be effective, numeracy skills must be taught and learned in settings that are both meaningful and memorable. (p. 11)

The list of numeracy skills (Figure 16.6) can be used to bring quantitative literacy experiences to your students.

Mathematician Jeff Knisley (2002) ties mathematical learning styles into the Kolb model:

- Concrete, reflective: Allegorizers prefer form over function and, thus, often ignore details; they address problems by seeking similar ap-

Arithmetic	Facility with simple mental arithmetic; estimating arithmetic calculations; reasoning with proportions; counting by indirection (combinatorics).
Data	Using information conveyed as data, graphs, and charts; drawing inferences from data; recognizing disaggregation as a factor in interpreting data.
Computers	Using spreadsheets, recording data, performing calculations, creating graphical displays, extrapolating, fitting lines or curves to data.
Modeling	Formulating problems, seeking patterns, and drawing conclusions; recognizing interactions in complex systems; understanding linear, exponential, multivariable, and simulation models; understanding the different rates of growth.
Statistics	Understanding the importance of variability; recognizing the differences between correlation and causation, between randomized experiments and observational studies, between finding no effect and finding no statistically significant effect (especially with small samples), and between statistical significance and practical importance (especially with large samples).
Chance	Recognizing that seemingly improbably coincidences are not uncommon; evaluating risks from available evidence; understanding the value of random samples.
Reasoning	Logical thinking; recognizing levels of rigor in methods of inference; checking hypotheses; exercising caution in generalizations.

Figure 16.6 Skills of Quantitative Literacy

Note. From Quantitative Literacy Design Team (2001). "The Case for Quantitative Literacy," in *Mathematics and Democracy: The Case for Quantitative Literacy,* L. A. Steen (Ed.), Princeton, NJ: The Woodrow Wilson National Fellowship Foundation, National Council on Education and the Disciplines, Mathematical Association of America. Reprinted with permission.

proaches in previous examples. The teacher's role is storyteller.

- Concrete, active: Integrators rely heavily on comparisons of new ideas to known ideas; they address problems by relying on their "common sense" insights. The teacher's role is guide.
- Abstract, reflective: Analyzers desire logical explanations and algorithms and solve problems with step-by-step progression that begins with the initial assumptions and concludes with the solution. The teacher's role is expert.
- Abstract, active: Synthesizers see concepts as tools for constructing new ideas and approaches; they solve problems by developing individual strategies and new approaches. The teacher's role is coach.

It is important to recognize the phenomenon of "math anxiety" when planning quantitative learning experiences. For whatever cultural reasons, people feel free to tell strangers or friends, "I just can't do math," when they would never think of telling the same people, "I just can't read" (or write). It is acceptable and even fashionable to be math deficient. Building quantitative elements into your course should be a natural learning experience leading to authentic goals.

Critical Thinking across the Curriculum

Critical thinking can be described as moving through the Bloom cognitive taxonomy from "remembering" toward "creating," developing along the Perry (1968/1970) scale from "dualism" toward "commitment," or growing in the Belenky, Clinchy, Goldberger, and Tarule (1986) scheme from "silence" toward becoming a "connected knower." Kurfiss (1988), provides eight principles for fostering critical thinking:

1. Critical thinking is a learnable skill.
2. Problems, questions, or issues are the point of entry into the subject and a source of motivation for sustained inquiry.
3. Successful courses balance the challenge to think critically with support tailored to students' developmental needs.
4. Courses should be assignment centered rather than text or lecture centered.
5. Students are required to formulate their ideas in writing or other observable means.
6. Students collaborate to stretch their thinking.
7. Teaching problem-solving skills nurtures metacognitive abilities.
8. Students' developmental needs are acknowledged and teachers help students achieve standards.

Every discipline, from art to zoology, requires critical-thinking skills that can be built into course design.

Transdisciplinarity

The challenges of the twenty-first century cannot be solved by the thinking of any one discipline. Transdisciplinary knowledge comes from discovering new territory within existing knowledge and tracing connections that were obscured by what was thought to be known within the narrow perspectives of the disciplines. This is an organic process that occurs from within—within a topic and within a group of people who are able to give up the comfort of their individual disciplines. As Albert Einstein said, "You can never solve a problem on the level on which it was created."

Transdisciplinary learning experiences require a radical move from traditionally accepted methods. Transdisciplinarity differs from interdisciplinary or multidisciplinary experiences that provide, but do not integrate, different methodologies. It requires a giant step away from the security of a known discipline, as well as trust in others and in an unknown process. Transdisciplinary courses (t-courses) focus the abilities of participants (instructors and students) from a variety of traditions on an unformed problem. They work together, integrating their methodological perspectives, to find solutions that one alone could not.

Transdisciplinary programs are found primarily in research areas confronting problems of social significance, such as smoking cessation, HIV/AIDS, hunger, and peace, where it is essential to bring together a variety of perspectives. The Claremont Graduate University (CGU) in Southern California has identified transdisciplinary abilities as essential for the development of future scholars and requires that all of its doctoral students complete a t-course within their first two years of study. Since its inception in 2000, the Preparing Future Faculty (PFF) Program at CGU has included transdisciplinary research in the fellows seminars on the "Academic Profession" and "Teaching and Learning in Higher Education." Each year, fellows, who are selected annually from all CGU disciplines, have worked together to research, present, and publish transdisciplinary scholarship on topics including stress during the academic career; the impact of nontenure track full-time academic positions on an academic career, students, institutions, and disciplines; and faculty lives at different types of institutions.

T-courses often are team taught by two or more instructors from a variety of disciplines in order to provide their different viewpoints, making it easier for students to bring their own ideas to the process. T-courses designed by PFF fellows include "New Orleans: Legacy and Promise" (to be taught by history, religion, cultural studies, economics, education, English, and psychology instructors) and "From Be-Bop to Hip-Hop: The Impact of the Harlem Renaissance on Current African-American Culture" (to be taught by psychology, education, history, and cultural studies instructors).

Four Clusters of Teaching Experiences

Grasha's (1996) four clusters of teaching and learning styles (see Figure 10.5) classify learning experiences as they are performed by instructors and provide appropriate learning experiences for a variety of types of learning styles.

Cluster 1 (Teaching Styles: Expert, Formal Authority; Learning Styles: Dependent, Participative, Competitive)

The learning experiences associated with cluster 1 are teacher centered and passive, but they can be effective if the teaching goals are to create excitement about the topic, model problem solving, provide otherwise unavailable material, or present the instructor's (or a guest's) personal opinions. We consider here three of them: lecturing, guest speakers, and technology-based presentations.

Lecturing

Organization of the lecture begins with the learning objectives being addressed. What will students know or be able to do after the lecture? In your preparation, create a roadmap for the students to know where the lecture will take them. The two biggest mistakes instructors make in lectures are including too much material and, therefore, lecturing too fast for listeners to understand. Include in your design conceptual pre-questions that ask students to focus on issues in a lec-

ture in order to help them retain information. You also can use flow charts, outlines, and lists of key terms (Lambiotte & Dansereau, 1992) to increase retention of information.

Bligh (2000) found that the lecture was no more effective in transmitting information than other methods, and that it was clearly less effective in promoting thought or changing attitudes. Costin (1972) found that the results of 58 studies showed that lecturing did not differ significantly from discussions in helping students learn facts and principles, but that discussion was superior to lecturing in developing problem-solving skills.

In your introduction, you need to get your students' attention, connect previous class topics to the lecture theme, and frame the topic in terms of course learning objectives. In the body of your lecture, create connections as you move from item to item. Providing an outline for students will help, but leave enough space for them to write their own notes. Include stories, examples, and pictures to flesh out your points. In your conclusion, repeat your main points, discuss how the material relates to the course objectives, and lay the groundwork for the next class session.

Presentation techniques are important for maintaining student interest: speak clearly; avoid distracting mannerisms, use effective speech techniques such as inflection, gestures, and pace; talk—do not read your lecture; be enthusiastic—start with a question, problem, or controversy; use humor; look at your listeners (Cashin, 1985).

There are alternative formats for lecturing that are essentially "mini" lectures broken up with active learning (clusters 3 and 4) activities such as short case studies or learning groups (pairs, trios) that "think-write-pair-share" on a question posed by the instructor. To create energy, enable more students to think about a topic; create community; and allow quiet students to express themselves in small, safe groups. A 50-minute class session might involve a 20-minute lecture that sets the stage for a 15-minute student activity and conclude with a 15-minute summary by the students and instructor. Longer class sessions might repeat the pattern multiple times.

Guest Speakers

Having a guest speaker can provide motivation for students to attend class and be involved with the topic. Outside experts, colleagues from other institutions, other faculty members, professional staff, and students from previous classes can bring fresh perspectives to the topic. It is important, of course, to prepare guests properly by explaining the learning objectives for the session and what role they will play. Provide guests with information about the composition of the class and the topics already covered. In addition, suggest various issues for guests to address, provide them with student-generated questions ahead of time, or have the students interview them outside of class (or by telephone or other technology) rather than ask them to give a lecture. Preparation is everything in having a guest speaker, so that class time is well used to achieve your goals for the course.

Technology-Based Presentations

Technology-based presentations, primarily the use of PowerPoint™ in classrooms, can have mixed results. You need only to view the hypothetical PowerPoint presentation by Abraham Lincoln (http://www.norvig.com/Gettysburg/) to realize what can be lost with the usual PowerPoint bullet points. On the other hand, there are times when PowerPoint is the best way to convey information. On his Web site, Steven H. Kaminski (2003) has posted "PowerPoint™ Presentations: The Good, the Bad and the Ugly" for his students to use. Figure 16.7 provides an adaptation of his advice for when to use and when not to use technology in a presentation.

Cluster 2 (Teaching Styles: Personal Model, Expert, Formal Authority; Learning Styles: Participant, Dependent, Competitive)

Cluster 2 learning experiences involve role modeling and coaching. We will consider team teaching as a "role model by illustration," where having more than one professor in the class provides students with the opportunity to observe people with different viewpoints "discussing alternate approaches" and "sharing thought processes" (Grasha, 1996, p. 234). Arranging a team-taught course is difficult because of the way institutions assign teaching "loads" and the amount of time it takes to design and conduct a course with more than one instructor. During the course, instructors need to meet frequently to debrief class sessions and plan for adapting the course design to the students and themselves. In addition, when team teaching, because they become students of each other, instructors risk exposing their own ignorance of the other teacher's discipline in front of the students. This provides the students with the in-

spiration to take the risk to try new approaches themselves, but can be uncomfortable for the instructors.

Robert Schaible and Betty Robinson have team taught a course on gender and work for many years. They self-consciously model collaborative behaviors and values that they want their students to adopt. Using an anonymous midterm survey, their students reported several benefits of having two teachers:

> [The two instructors] *feed off each other. There are times when they both have different opinions and that gives us a better way to look at different situations.*
>
> [Having two instructors] *opens the class up to several ideas/perspectives, sometimes conflicting with one another.*
>
> [Having two instructors] *helps us to understand a broader perspective—neither one is always right or wrong—we see that more than one can work better than one.*
>
> *Since they sometimes differed, this allowed me to realize I could differ from both of them. Thus I was given freedom to explore the material.*
>
> *It's easier to speak up in class because they encouraged each other as well as us, making the class more open.*
>
> *It's easier to ask a question, knowing that each professor will have their own answers reflecting their own disciplines and opinions.* (Schaible & Robinson, 1995, p. 14)

Barkley, Clifton, deCourcy, and Kloos (1998) found that interdisciplinary team teaching increases the likelihood that students will:

- develop the perspective of more than one discipline through which to view the world;
- develop an enhanced consciousness of self and other;
- come to see faculty members as part of the learning community; and
- learn effective interaction between disciplines in a conversational, civil model of exchange. (p. 89)

They found that "interdisciplinary learning better addresses the complexity of the world problems we face than traditional learning models. Furthermore, team-taught learning better matches the most fruitful problem-solving approaches that are being practiced in the world of work and service. . . ." (p. 99).

When to Use PowerPoint™

Communication delivered over *multiple channels* is more efficient than communication over a single channel. Multiple channels make it more likely that the whole message will be received. An appropriate picture adds another channel. A picture *aids in memory* by making a visual connection to an abstract idea. PowerPoint™ makes it *easy to create visuals,* and, by using a template, makes it easy to be consistent.

Use PowerPoint™ when it makes sense and resist the temptation to use it too often.

Use PowerPoint™ primarily for conveying a simple, generally informative message to a large group of people. It falters with deliberative messages or discussions with smaller groups.

Considerations

It's too easy to create slides. Because you can crank them out quickly, you make far more than are appropriate for the presentation.

It wastes time. You can use up precious time tweaking a presentation.

It takes too much control away from the presenter. It makes it too easy to start the presentation with PowerPoint™ instead of starting with ideas and using PowerPoint™ to reinforce them.

It makes for ugly presentations. Most people are not trained in design. The computer puts tools in average hands that were once reserved only for artists.

It can actually impede attention. Military analysts conjecture that recent appropriations from Capitol Hill have stalled because Congress cannot decipher the Army's complex and tedious slides.

It lends itself to unnecessary competition. Presenters—particularly students—become distracted with "dueling PowerPoint™."

It does not lend itself to spontaneous discussions in the classroom or boardroom. It is heavily scripted and is not a tool for discovery.

It does not handle text well. The general rule for PowerPoint™ text is no more than three lines of text on a slide and no more than 6 words per line. Therefore, if you try to put a lot of text in a presentation, you have to move through a lot of slides. The rapid movement does nothing to aid the presentation. Instead it detracts from the message.

It too easily becomes a replacement for the presenter, not a reinforcement. Instead of a visual aid for the speaker, the speaker becomes an audio aid for the slides. This strips the presentation of some of its most essential appeals.

Presenters rely too much on the slides for structure. Clear structure should still be part of the verbal presentation even with visual aids. The aids should reinforce the structure, not replace it. This is particularly troublesome for student presentations since students need to learn how to communicate structure verbally without visuals. If they rely on visuals for structure, they never learn how to do it themselves.

Presenters fail to establish the connections necessary to make their message memorable. They often rely too much on the visual slide to make the connection and neglect repetition, examples, metaphors and other devices that make a message memorable.

Presenters fail to establish ethos, their most powerful appeal. Ethos is the personal appeal of the speaker. It is classified by Aristotle as an "artistic proof" that the speaker fashions in his presentation. It involves both verbal and nonverbal elements of the message and must be carefully managed for a presentation to succeed. With PowerPoint™, however, many of the elements that establish ethos are blunted or negated. Speakers don't look at the audience and the audience doesn't look at the speaker. The subtle nonverbal cues are lost such as eye contact, posture, etc. Presentations tend to be read off the slide or handouts, flattening delivery.

Figure 16.7 When & How to Use PowerPoint™ and Why You May Not Want To

Note. From *PowerPoint Presentations: The Good, the Bad and the Ugly,* by S. H. Kaminski, 2003, http://www.shkaminski.com/Classes/Handouts/powerpoint.htm (retrieved August 2005). Copyright 2004 by Kaminski. Adapted with permission.

Cluster 3 (Teaching Styles: Facilitator, Personal Model, Expert; Learning Styles: Collaborative, Participant, Independent)

Cluster 3 learning experiences involve active student participation. Designing and implementing these activities is more difficult and time-consuming than writing out and reading a lecture. Foremost of the cluster 3 experiences is conducting productive discussions. Also important are problem-based learning (PBL) and case studies and peer teaching.

Discussions

Useful class discussions are based on well-designed questions, which serve specific purposes in discussions; assignments such as essays and journals; and tests. We ask our students questions for different reasons: Do you want to be sure that they have read assignments? Is there a need to calculate a precise answer? Do you want to decide whether to involve a large number of them in investigating "discussable" ideas? Whichever your purpose, how you design your questions can help or hinder your students in reaching the goal. Andrews (1980) investigated how the verbal structure of a question contributes to the quality of classroom discussion. By analyzing audiotapes of actual classroom discussions, Andrews categorized the verbal structure of questions and counted the number of individual student contributions, the number of students involved, and the number of student-follows-student sequences to determine which types of questions generated more discussion. The results, shown in Figure 16.8, show that questions that were divergent, at a higher cognitive level, straightforward, and structured resulted in higher levels of each of the three categories of responses.

There are two important concepts in creating a good discussion: safety and discussability. As Andrews (1980) advises, "Don't be seduced by 'pure' freedom" (p. 155). Unless students are very interested, prepared, and mature they will get lost in questions that are too broad. Limit the scope of the question to a particularly important element. Questions with built-in structure generate more discussion than unfocused questions. Students will be more open if they feel safe to participate.

Questions must be discussable. It is not ethical to pose a question as though students can discover their own answers when you really are asking them to guess at what you want. Questions can be convergent or divergent. A *convergent* question has single or multiple *correct* answers. Some analysis or inference may be necessary, but examination of the material will lead straightforwardly to the conclusion. Convergent questions can be comparisons, cause-and-effect statements, and other application of analysis-level thinking. *Divergent* questions, on the other hand, are "discussable"; they require students to reason to their own conclusions and defend them. Therefore, divergent questions generate more responses. It is very important to be clear to your students which type of question you are asking.

Problem-Based Learning and Case Studies

PBL began in the 1960s and first was used by medical and business schools to teach their students how to solve complex problems. PBL has spread to undergraduate courses, with great success in engaging and motivating students (Eck, 2000). The success of PBL depends on the design of the problem used. David Chapman (2000, pp. 75–78) identifies the motivational aspects of well-designed problems:

- Familiarity: "Students respond naturally to problems that are within the realm of their experience" (p. 75).
- Relevance: "This relevance may be based on the students' current needs or any needs they anticipate in the immediate future" (75–76).
- Dramatic appeal: "Problems can frequently be enhanced by the dramatic elements that make up a good story" (p. 76).
- Significance: "The knowledge that the information students were collecting would be valued by someone other than the teacher added the element of significance to the assignment. This proved to be a powerful motivational force" (pp. 76–77).
- Authenticity: "The use of real-world problems is considered one of the predominant features of PBL" (pp. 77–78).
- Group collaboration: "Students who participate in the group process often feel more enthusiastic about their assigned task and show greater levels of commitment to the project than students who do not have similar interaction with fellow students" (p. 78).

Chapman also identifies factors that detract from student motivation in the PBL classroom:

Rank	Responses (Student Statements)	Question Types & Examples	Reasoning
7th (Fewest Responses)	1.45	Quiz Show: Question calls for facts, definitions, and description of events. Examples: What was the name of that institution? He talks about envying one character. Who was it?	These are convergent, low level questions that call for brief responses.
6th	1.95	Analytic Convergent: These questions imply that there is a single correct answer. The instructor has a single endpoint in mind which the student can be expected to identify. They usually involve comparisons, cause and effect statements, drawing of straightforward inferences from limited material, but for a desired end by the instructor. Examples: So, in this story, when's the point of truth for Kurtz? What was the most important reason for the revolution's failure?	Although some analysis or inference is necessary, there is a single end-point which the instructor has in mind and which students are expected to identify.
5th	2.50	Shotgun: A series of questions all at once that may not even relate to each other. Examples: So, we're talking about the act that everybody's roles are changing, how—we've mentioned religion and education, how did religion and education during this period affect these changes, or how did the changes affect the kind of religion and education people had? . . . Let's start with religion . . . have women always had a sort of divine place in religion? How do you interpret what the narrator tells you about the hero? What do you make of his return from law school? Why did he decide he didn't really expect too much?	Whatever the quality of the individual questions, the fact that they are fired off together leads to confusion by the students at what they should answer.
4th	2.60	General Invitation: Broad, vague, and often defined by a conventionally obvious unit of the course, "the lecture," or "the book." Examples: What about the lecture? Any comments on Plato?	No structure to guide students; students may "freeze" in confusion of the freedom they are offered.
3rd	4.29	Focal: Ordered around an issue that calls for decisions. The instructor poses a limited number (2–3) and asks students to take stands which they are to justify during discussion or on a test. Examples: Is Ivan Illych a victim of society, or did he create his problems by his own choices? So where is this wild boy better off? In the forest where he started, or in civilization being socialized?	Safety provided by alternatives posed by instructor; calls for higher order thinking to justify choices.

Figure 16.8   Andrews Question Typography and Results

Rank	Responses (Student Statements)	Question Types & Examples	Reasoning
2nd	4.88	Brainstorm: Any and all ideas or solutions in response to a specific question or problem. The primary subject is thematic, with the subject matter being less tightly focused. Examples: What possibilities are there for refuge in *A Farewell to Arms*? What kinds of things is Hamlet questioning? Not just in his soliloquy, but broadly, throughout the whole play?	Any and all responses allowed in answer to a specific question or problem. Structure provided by theme.
1st (Most Responses)	5.08	Playground: An invitation to explore. The instructor designates a specific intellectual sphere (the "playground") and then gives students the widest possible latitude in approaching it. Examples: (Instructor reads a sentence from the novel under study): Well, that's a very rich sentence . . . there's a lot there . . . OK, what's there? Can we make any generalizations about the play as a whole, from the nature of the opening lines?	Provides safety in specific intellectual sphere and an invitation to explore within that sphere. Leaves open the concept, category, or theme the student will use to make sense of the raw material offered.

Figure 16.8 (continued)

Note. From Andrews, J. D. W. (Fall/Winter, 1980). Verbal structure of teacher questions: Its impact on class discussion. *POD Quarterly, 2*(3&4), 129–163.

- Overly complex problems: "Open-ended problems can be exhilarating for students, but they also can be overwhelming" (p. 79).
- Overly determined problems: "If the problem is simply a matter of applying a formula, students may find the problem-solving activity to be a waste of time and effort" (p. 79).
- Formal group reports: "If PBL is intended to overcome student passivity and increase motivation, it should place the emphasis on collaborative activities, not class presentations" (p. 80).

The case method is a subset of PBL that is easier to use because the "problem" is well defined, rather than open-ended (although there are multiple paths to any solution). Figure 16.9 presents the types and attributes of materials used in case studies. The "case material in effect becomes a 'trigger' for helping students to analyze and synthesize information, apply concepts and principles in a course, solve problems and make decisions, and generally to identify and examine broader implication of the content" (Grasha, 1996, p. 285). Grasha (1996,

p. 287) recommends these processes to make cases more effective:

- "State the general goals you want the case to accomplish and communicate these to students."
- "Allow participants adequate time to read the case and to develop a response to your questions."
- "Requiring students to do a written preliminary analysis insures that people have read the case and supporting materials [e.g., textbook assignments, outside readings, other materials] and have thought about the issues involved."
- "Place the responsibility for responding on the students."
- "Keep any content points you make short, specific and to the point."
- "Always provide a summary of key issues raised and any resolutions of issues that were obtained as part of a wrap-up at the end of a session."

Examples of Case Materials

- Films or videotapes on a topic
- A business plan
- Description of a marketing problem a company faced and solved
- Current research study
- Classic research study
- Narrative description of some problems or concern.
- A nonfiction account of a historical or other important event
- Magazine or newspaper article
- Book dealing with a topic relevant to a course
- Instructor designed story or narrative of an issue
- Minutes of a regulatory body
- Description of a mystery or puzzle in a field
- A story about discovery and invention in a discipline
- Television show
- Advertisement on television, radio, newspaper, or magazine
- Popular movie
- Clinical case study
- Narrative description of how a new process or procedure in a discipline was invented, developed or used
- A series of photographs or works of art on a particular topic

Characteristics of Good Case Materials

- Engage the interest and imagination of students
- Contain examples of and the use of content students must acquire
- Provide interesting examples of principles and concepts
- Do not have simple answers and thus are more complicated than they appear on the surface. Good case materials often contain engaging unknowns, paradoxes, and other complications.
- Can be analyzed to produce a deeper understanding of issues
- Allow for some degree of resolution of the issues raised in the case through analysis, synthesis, and the discussion of alternative paths to obtain a resolution
- Are at an appropriate level of complexity and difficulty for the students
- Can be partitioned into themes, parts, or issues that can be individually and jointly analyzed
- Allow engaging questions to be written about the content to help guide and direct the students' attention to important issues
- Are amenable to discussion in small and large groups
- Sustain the interest of students [and the instructor] for one or more class periods

---

Figure 16.9 Examples and Characteristics of Materials That Can Increase Success in Case Study Exercises

Note. From *Teaching with Style: A Practical Guide to Enhancing Learning by Understanding Teaching and Learning Styles* (p. 286), by A. F. Grasha, 1996, Claremont, CA: Alliance Publishers (www.iats.com). Copyright 1996 by Alliance. Reprinted with permission.

Peer Teaching

The final cluster 3 learning experience we consider here is peer teaching, in which students become teachers for a particular topic. An individual student can present to the entire class, or several students can present to their small groups all on the same topic on the same day. Making the teaching experience useful for student learning requires good design and effective preparation of the student teacher. Grasha (1996, pp. 312–313) recommends the following:

- "*Student teachers need time to prepare.* Thus, the assignment of topics should be made early in the term. It is also helpful for the instructor to meet with the student teachers a week or so before the session" (pp. 312–313).

- "*During the class session, the instructor for the class can sit outside of the groups to check on what is going on and after the discussions solicits questions and comments about the content*" (p. 313).
- "*To insure that quality instruction takes place, a teacher must closely monitor the work of the student teachers.* They should receive feedback on their performance and given tips on how they could have improved the quality of their presentation" (p. 313).

Cluster 4 (Teaching Styles: Delegator, Facilitator, Expert; Learning Styles: Independent, Collaborative, Participant)

Cluster 4 learning experiences include collaborative and cooperative group work and debates. They are the most active and student centered of all of the clusters. To teach these experiences effectively, Grasha (1996) recommends doing the following:

- Organize class sessions and course activities and tasks around a variety of student-centered instructional processes.
- Consult with students individually or in small groups as they prepare to participate in classroom activities and tasks [e.g., getting material together for a debate, developing questions for a learning pairs' activity].
- Work with students who are engaged in independent study processes such as research projects, position papers, guided readings. (p. 267)

Collaborative and Cooperative Group Work

Many faculty members use small groups in their classroom without considering the structural differences among different types of assignments. Philip Cottell, Jr. (1996) explains how they relate:

Collaborative learning is the broader concept and may encompass any kind of collaboration between student as well as various other forms of collaboration, such as team-taught courses, learning community models, and other interactions between faculty and students. Many regard cooperative learning as a more structured, and hence more focused, form of collaborative learning. Others view collaborative learning and cooperative learning as lying on a continuum, with collaborative learning being the least structured and cooperative learning the most structured. . . . Underlying both is a basic respect for students—regardless of their ethnic, intellectual, educational, or social backgrounds—and a belief in their potential for academic success. . . . Advocates of both cooperative learning and collaborative learning share a belief that learning is an active, constructive process. . . . [T]he role of the instructor changes from that of a deliverer of information to a facilitator of learning. This does not mean that faculty members abdicate their responsibilities to students; rather, it means that they assume different roles in the class and in their relationships with students. (pp. 1–2)

Barbara Millis (1991), well-known author, and sometimes coauthor with Philip Cottell, of books and articles on cooperative learning, has connected the process with the *Seven Principles of Good Practice in Undergraduate Education*, discussed in chapter 14:

1. *Good Practice Encourages Student-Faculty Contact.* "Faculty constantly monitor groups' process by sitting with the students" (p. 140).
2. *Good Practice Encourages Cooperation Among Students.* "Two features, positive interdependence and individual accountability, distinguish cooperative learning from collaborative group work. Positive interdependence means that students—because of carefully structured mutual rewards—have goals, division of tasks, role interdependence, or group vested interest in working collaboratively together" (p. 141).
3. *Good Practice Encourages Active Learning.* "By its very nature, cooperative learning engenders active learning. Students engage in animated discussions as they carry out structured class assignments. . . ." (p. 141).
4. *Good Practice Gives Prompt Feedback.* "With structured small group work, students have ample opportunity to receive continuous and immediate feedback from their peers" (p. 142).
5. *Good Practice Emphasizes Time on Task.* "Faculty unfamiliar with cooperative learning may believe mistakenly that small group work is

time consuming. This is not necessarily true if the tasks are timed and structured and the desired outcome is student learning tied to the course objectives" (p. 142).

6. *Good Practice Communicates High Expectations.* "Because cooperative learning emphasizes peer tutoring, collaborative learning, and positive social skills, it automatically signals to students that their abilities are valued and respected" (p. 143).

7. *Good Practice Respects Diverse Talents and Ways of Learning.* "Cooperative learning supplements, but does not replace, other methods of classroom delivery . . . resulting in a diverse array of teaching-learning approaches" (p. 143).

Instructors have five roles in using formal cooperative-learning groups (Johnson, Johnson, & Smith, 1991, p. 58):

1. Specifying the objectives for the lesson, including both academic learning objectives and social skills objectives

2. Making preinstruction decisions: establishing group size, assigning students to groups, arranging the room, planning instructional materials to promote interdependence, and assigning roles to ensure interdependence

3. Explaining the tasks and goal structure to the students: clearly stating objectives; defining relevant concepts and procedures; explaining the criteria for success; and structuring positive interdependence, individual accountability, and group cooperation

4. Monitoring and intervening in group activities including observing and keeping track of student behavior, assisting with tasks, and stepping in to teach social skills

5. Evaluating learning and processing interaction by providing closure to the lesson, evaluating the quality and quantity of students' learning, and processing group functioning

Debates
Debates can be "substantive," such as a court trial, or "educational," such as the debates that Aristotle carried on with his students (Combs & Bourne, 1994).

Some of the benefits of classroom debates found by Schnoeder and Ebert (1983) are as follows:

- Limit the extent to which instructor bias may be imposed on a course.
- Force students to surpass their own biases.
- Compel students to do research, which is an indispensable part of reflective decision making (Ehninger & Brochriede, 1972).
- Require that students discard the crutch of memorization.
- Motivate students to perform well, to impress their peers.
- Provide a change from traditional teaching methods; students participate actively in the learning process.

Debates can use a traditional format of small teams each supporting one side of an argument, or a full-class format in which each student is prepared to support either side. Student roles in a debate could be presenter, logical thinker, challenger, consultant, or observer (Grasha, 1996, pp. 320, 323).

TEACHING AND LEARNING OUTSIDE OF CLASS

Many studies of student success (Astin, 1977; Bowen, 1977; Pace, 1979) have found that "students learn more when they are actively engaged in various aspects of college life" (Kuh, 1991). Three types of outside-of-class learning experiences are involved:

1. Informal interactions with faculty "after class" such as meetings in the hallway, laboratory, library, residence hall, or union and collaboration on research

2. Service learning or internship programs connected to specific courses

3. Co-op programs in which students spend alternating semesters on campus and working in the community

Service-learning programs and internships are a popular way to connect authentic experiences to course content. Most large universities and some colleges have offices to work with faculty members who want to include off-campus work with their courses.

ONLINE LEARNING EXPERIENCES

How do we create teaching experiences on-line that lead to deep and sustained learning by students? Hacker and Niederhauser (2000) identify five principles, backed with "particularly strong empirical support," that promote "ways in which the online classroom can be even more conducive than traditional classrooms to using these learning principles" (p. 53):

1. use active participation by students to "construct deep explanations, justifications, and reasons for what they think and do";
2. "effective use of examples";
3. require collaborative problem solving and "metacognitive understanding of how, when and why to use problem-solving strategies";
4. "use feedback that is commensurate with performance"; and
5. embed within the instruction "motivational components that enhance self-efficacy and perceived challenge."

Designing effective online courses involves a partnership between the faculty member and an instructional technologist. Doolittle and Chambers (2004) note that "at each new technological turn (radio, television, cable television, the Internet), a new age of learning and discovery has been proclaimed" (p. 1). Palloff and Pratt (1999) state:

> The shift to computer-mediated distance learning poses enormous challenges to instructors and their institutions. Many faculty members believe that the online classroom is no different from the traditional one—that the approaches that work face to face will work when learners are separated from them and from each other by time and distance. However, when the only connection we have to our students is through words on a screen, we must pay attention to many issues that we take for granted in the face-to-face classroom. (p. xiv)

Palloff and Pratt (1999) add that they "have seen many distance education programs in which the instructor posts lectures and attempts to control the learning outcomes by directing and dominating the process" (pp. 30–31), creating a cluster 1 type of experience. Desired outcomes from an "online community" are as follows:

- Active interaction involving both course content and personal communication
- Collaborative learning evidenced by comments directly from student to student rather than student to instructor
- Socially constructed meaning evidenced by agreement or questioning, with the intent to achieve agreement on issues of meaning
- Sharing of resources among students
- Expressions of support and encouragement exchanged between students, as well as willingness to critically evaluate the work of others (p. 32)

Faculty members report that the preparation and maintenance time needed to deliver an online class is two to three times greater than to deliver a face-to-face class. Figure 16.10 shows a time comparison of an online versus a face-to-face class for one week. The time involved also varies in either type of course depending on the number of students, comfort with technology, support services, and the amount of discussion versus lecture involved. Even instructors who have taught many times in online environments depend on quick and efficient technical support during their courses. Designing an online or hybrid course takes more time and collaboration than classroom-based courses, especially the first time they are planned. And each time equipment is "upgraded" there is another learning curve to climb. Online courses benefit from close collaboration between the instructor and technical support staff. The instructor needs to be certain that all students have access to the technology they need, and it is an absolute necessity that a technical person be available at all times whom the students and instructor can contact immediately if there is a problem accessing the Web site.

According to Tisha Bender (2003), online learning can support nonlinear learning through threaded discussions, in which student postings are sorted by the topic addressed rather than by the time received, and

Time Comparisons of an Online Versus a Face-to-Face Class for One Week

Instructor Activity	Face-to-Face Class	Online Class
Preparation	2 hours per week to: Review assigned reading Review lecture material Review and prepare in-class activities	2 hours per week to: Review assigned reading Prepare discussion questions and "lecture" material in the form of a paragraph or two
Class Time	2½ hours per week of assigned class time	2 hours **daily** to: Read student posts Respond to student posts
Follow-up	2 to 3 hours per week for: Individual contact with students Reading student assignments	2 to 3 hours per week for: Individual contact with students via e-mail and phone Reading student assignments
Totals for Week	6½ to 7½ hours per week	18 to 19 hours per week

Figure 16.10   Instructor Teaching Activities

Note. From *Building Communities in Cyberspace: Effective Strategies for the Online Classroom* (p. 50), by R. M. Palloff and K. Pratt, 1999, San Francisco: Jossey-Bass. Copyright 1999 by Jossey-Bass. Adapted with permission.

hypertext, the ability to jump to any site around the Web. She recommends that "the online instructor should allow for freedom within learning to make concepts meaningful, realizing this can often be brought about by nonlinear, associative means. The instructor also must be a great facilitator in pulling together disparate strands of conversations, expertly weaving the different threads of expressed thought together to make a cohesive body of knowledge, which can move forward in a linear fashion until it naturally starts to branch out again" (p. 33). Online environments can accommodate a wide variety of learning styles and personalities. Bender (2003) states:

For example, some students may be shy or reluctant to speak in front of a group on campus, might open up more freely when in front of their computer screens, and the reverse may be true for other students. Some students do not learn well from lectures, and many students actually discover their own voice for the first time

when working online. Furthermore, providing the means of communicating information through a variety of media and environments might help students to be able to engage in more class activities than if it was solely one type of environmental forum. . . . A . . . third advantage is that the different phases of learning can occur in different environments, which has important implications on instructional design. Kolb's (1984) Learning Cycle suggests that there is a continuous cycle of four processes when learning takes place: experience, reflection, conceptualization, and planning. The campus class might be the most suitable environment for gaining an experience (such as watching a film, seeing an exhibit, or hearing a reading) and possibly might also be the best place for planning, whereas sandwiched in between, the online class, due to its asynchronous environment, might be the most appropriate forum for reflection and conceptualization. (p. xvii)

SECTION THREE

Assessing Learning

NOW THAT YOU HAVE OPERATIONALIZED THE HOPES AND DREAMS IN teaching goals and learning objectives, and designed learning experiences for specific students, the next step is to specify how you will know how well the students achieve the objectives. Students must be assessed only on what they have been taught, and at the same level as their learning activities. Students will focus their time on what they perceive will be assessed. And what you assess should be what is most important (as specified in the learning objectives), and your assessment should be done in ways in which they can best show what they have learned.

The chapters in this section discuss setting up grading schemes and policies, connecting assessment to the course objectives, building in low-stakes feedback, and designing tests and assignments that can assess student achievement. The focusing tool for assessment is the learning objective.

CHAPTER 17

Grading Schemes and Policies

LEARNING OBJECTIVES

Readers of this chapter will be able to:

- Describe advantages and disadvantages of norm-referenced and criterion-based grading schemes.
- Describe policies for missed tests and late papers appropriate to course learning objectives.
- Design an appropriate grading scheme for their own course.

YOUR CHOICE OF THE COURSE GRADING SCHEME AND testing and grading policies defines the importance of course activities. Your decisions will include whether students will be compared with each other or with a fixed standard and whether or not tests can be retaken and papers handed in later than the original due date. Most important, setting your grading parameters will determine how your students will spend their time during the course.

GRADING SCHEMES

The assessment of student learning begins with your values. Grading is most effective when it is integrated with student learning activities and has a clear, explicitly stated purpose. Assessment works best when it is ongoing, with continual feedback to the learner. Through assessment, instructors meet responsibilities to both students and the public. A well-designed grading plan saves time, makes the process fair and consistent, and explains to students what they need to learn. A clear plan also helps students to evaluate their own work and give each other constructive feedback, and it saves instructors from having to explain what they "really wanted" after work is handed in. It can help sequence

courses and can form the basis for departmental and institutional assessment.

Grades serve many purposes. They are depended on to be a valid, fair, and trustworthy judgment about the quality of the students' work. A grade is a communication to students, as well as to employers, graduate schools, and others. It can be a highly emotional communication. The grading plan affects how students study, how much time they spend on various subjects, and how involved they are in the course. A grade on a test or an assignment helps to mark transitions, bring closure, and focus effort for both students and teachers.

Grading is based on judgment, similar to the process of a jury. The clearer your "laws," the more likely your students will be able to follow them.

Walvoord and Anderson (1998) say to "abandon the false hopes" of grading: total objectivity, total agreement, and one-dimensional student motivation for learning. They recommend several time-saving strategies, including separating commenting and grading and using them singly or in combination according to your purpose, using only as many grade levels as you need, not wasting time on careless student work, asking students to organize their work for your efficiency, delegating the work, and using technology to save time and enhance results. To grade effectively, they recommend identifying the most valuable kinds of learning in a course, constructing exams and assignments that will test that learning, setting standards and criteria, guiding students' learning, and implementing changes in teaching that are based on information from the grading process.

The two major types of grading schemes are norm referenced (grading on a curve) and criterion based (meeting a set standard). Each type has both advantages and disadvantages. The advantages of grading on a curve are that it can discriminate among individuals, regardless of the overall ability level of the group, and will provide an even or predetermined grade distribution. It is the most popular educational measurement and, therefore, requires minimal faculty training. The disadvantages of norm-referenced grading are that it is based on a relative standard that changes with the performance of each group and assesses students' status in relation to one another, not on their proficiency in subject matter. It leads to the self-fulfilling prophecy that some students will be high achievers, many will do moderately well, and a few will fail. Grading on a curve assumes a normal distribution of activity, but teaching is a purposeful activity. Because students are ranked against each other, curving grades encourages competition, instead of cooperation. It increases students' anxiety about grades because grades cannot be determined until the end of the course. Additionally, it is demotivating for most students, because they achieve well on assignments but receive a poor grade depending on the skill of the competition. With norm-referenced grading, incompetent yet top-ranked students may get high grades. And, at the other extreme, a certain number of students must fail, even if they perform well.

Criterion-referenced grading has many advantages. For example, assessment is based on comparison against a standard, not on the performance of others. It is useful in selecting individuals who can perform at a given competence level because it indicates what students have learned, not their status in comparison to others. Criterion grading also can assess both teaching and learning if valid criterion levels and entering prerequisites exist. In addition, grade distribution is unaffected by an unusual number of high or low achievers in one class. It is therefore motivating for most students because all can earn top grades and success depends solely on actual achievement.

The disadvantages of criterion-referenced grading include that it is unfamiliar, thus requiring explanation,

defense, and faculty training. It also is difficult to establish criterion levels. And, because there is no automatic "weeding out" of a certain percentage of students, all students may fail or all may earn top grades.

If a course is developmental, the grading scheme needs to measure what the student has achieved by the end of the course, compensating for early failures or slow starts. If it is unit based, in which each unit is equally important, the units are not highly cumulative and no final exam or project can measure students' total achievement. In developing your grading system, you need to consider whether your students are most powerfully motivated by a grading system that gives early, firm grades and rewards strong work no matter where it appears in the term; or by a system that allows early failure and slow starts and/or allows a great deal of individual flexibility, student choice, and student participation in establishing expectations.

TESTING AND GRADING POLICIES

Like the rest of the course design process, grading policies must be focused on student learning. Some institutions have very detailed policies specifying what student groups may be excused from taking scheduled tests because of school events; others leave the policies up to the individual instructor. The most controversial policies are the ones that relate to missed tests and late papers. These range from "no problem" to refusal to provide alternative opportunities. Once again, instructors need to consider themselves first, particularly the time available for test design, provision, and grading. That time varies from discipline to discipline. Some fields, such as calculus, have a large test bank of questions that are more easily graded, and instructors find it easier to provide additional testing opportunities. Other tests, such as those involving essay questions, are more difficult to create and to grade. Class size matters, as well. Whereas it would be possible to grade 10 essays overnight and provide timely feedback, it would not be possible to read and grade 50.

The case of "Beth's Midterm" (Fisch, 1989), shown in Figure 17.1, poses issues that can help clarify which policies will provide the most support for student learning. What would be the best answer to Beth when she asks to postpone the test? Why? Would it make a difference if Beth were the top A++ student last term? If the members of the debate team really had expected to be back earlier because they had never before made it to the semifinals, but this year they had not only made it to the final but had won and now were the state champions? If Beth were a major in the department, the professor were her advisor, and she needed a good grade to go on to graduate school? If the course had a grading system in which the comprehensive final would include all of the material covered on the midterm? Your answers to these questions will help determine the parameters of the grading policies appropriate to the course.

There are several ways to avoid the conflicts created by missed tests and late papers. Some of the most popular are to give frequent exams and count only the highest scores on a specified number of them, give choices to students about how they will be tested, and provide a

---

Beth's Midterm

As I hurried down the corridor to my 11 o'clock class I glanced at my watch—a couple of minutes to spare, plenty of time to rearrange the chairs and pass out the test. I looked up and saw Beth Winston, a student from my 3 o'clock class, standing in the doorway.

What now, I wondered. Beth had made only a C in my introductory course last spring, but I had the impression she could be a much better student if she only paid more attention to academics; she always seemed to be cutting corners. I didn't dislike her, but I always felt a little uneasy about her. At times she could be a bit abrasive.

"Dr. Spencer, I want to talk with you about this afternoon's midterm," Beth stated.

"Yes it is this afternoon . . ." I replied, trying to mask the irritation I was feeling.

"I'd like to take it on Monday," she said.

"Why?" I asked.

"Well, we just got back from the debate trip yesterday, and I haven't had much time to prepare for it," she said.

"Beth, when you told me last week about the trip, you said you'd only be absent Monday. I wondered where you were when we had the review Wednesday." I felt an edge creeping into my voice despite my efforts to suppress it.

"I know," she said, "but I thought we'd be back sooner. I didn't realize we'd be gone six days."

"This exam's been scheduled since the beginning of the term. You knew that. You've got to learn to fit extracurriculars around your academic commitments."

"Debate's academic. I'm going to law school."

"Didn't you take your books with you and study on the trip?"

"Yeah. But you can't get much studying done traveling in a van. I just need to work on it some more."

"I don't think it would be fair to the other students to give you an extra weekend to study. They've managed to live within our schedule."

"But the debate trip's an official school function; the absence is approved, just like athletics. Football players get to take make-up exams if . . ."

"What happens to football players is not relevant here," I interrupted.

"I think it is. I think you're just not treating me fairly."

I looked at my watch anxiously. "Beth, I've got a class right now. On the basis of what you've told me, I don't think you've got a case."

"But you keep saying you want to help us do well. And you said right in the syllabus that you'd arrange a make-up if we gave you advance notice. . . ."

"I said I'd consider it if there were a very good reason. And a couple of hours is hardly advance notice, Beth."

"You let me do it last year."

Beth just glared at me. Tears were beginning to well in her eyes.

"I think you'd better plan on taking the exam today," I said as I glanced at my watch again, "and you've got four hours to get ready for it."

The class bell rang. As I stepped into the classroom, Beth turned and stomped down the corridor.

In the leisure of hindsight, I look back on this incident and ponder about the way I handled it. Was my response reasonable under the circumstances? Did I over-react? Did I treat Beth unfairly? Was I biased against her? Did I overpower her? How might I have responded more appropriately and/or more effectively? Was my behavior ethical?

Figure 17.1   A Classroom Scenario That Poses Issues Regarding Testing Policy

Note. From *Beth's Midterm*, by L. Fisch, 1989, October, paper presented at the annual meeting of the Professional and Organizational Development (POD) Network in Higher Education, Jeckyll Island, GA. Copyright 1990 Linc. Fisch. Used by permission. With appropriate attribution to the source, this material may be duplicated and used for nonprofit educational purposes.

time near the end of the course for students to make up any exam they may have missed.

The question of late papers is more difficult if you are faced with a time crunch for providing feedback. Having a number of short assignments rather than one or two high-stakes papers will allow the opportunity of dropping an assignment. A policy of taking points away from a score if a paper is late indicates that you are able to assess a late paper. This gives a mixed message to students about the importance of the due date. And, if you are going to grade on promptness, you need to teach time management skills that go into constructing a paper of the type you have assigned. This might include research methods, data recording, note taking, report formats, word processing, and correct citations for your discipline.

The other "hot spot" in course policies relates to "participation." Separate attendance and participation. If you require attendance, be clear about why you do so and how you will record it. Specify exactly what activities are seen as participation and include them in the learning objectives (LOs) and learning activities. If by participation you mean asking questions in class, learning objectives may state, for example, *Students will be able to*

Create appropriate questions on the material.
Bring questions on the material to class.
Provide copies of questions to the instructor and other students.

Learning activities would include teaching students how to read the text and how to design questions at the appropriate Bloom level. There is no reason to assume that students would be able to do either when they enter the course. Of course, if you want students to participate orally during class discussions, you will need to provide them with instruction on public speaking and group participation. See Figure 21.1 (p. 99) for a rubric to assess participation.

CHAPTER 18

From Goals to Assessment

LEARNING OBJECTIVES

Readers of this chapter will be able to:

- Translate teaching goals into an evaluation plan.
- Place evaluation plan into Blueprint segment with the teaching goals and learning objectives.

ONCE YOU HAVE DETERMINED YOUR TEACHING GOALS and learning objectives, and created the course learning experiences, creating an evaluation plan and choosing assessment methods becomes relatively straightforward. The elements that have gone into your design to this point make clear what students need to know and be able to do. Now you can determine whether that will be through written or oral communication or by demonstration. It is at this point that you can look back at the objectives and activities and fine-tune them to meet the assessment plan. The Blueprint segments in Figure 18.1 show the progression to assessment.

Introductory Psychology Course

TG = Teaching Goal   LO = Learning Objective   LE = Learning Experience   EP = Evaluation Plan

SEGMENT
Knowledge Dimension: Factual Knowledge
Cognitive Process: Remember

TG	Students will learn the facts and concepts of twentieth-century psychology.
LO	Students completing this course will be able to list the five most influential psychologists of the twentieth century.
LE	Students will read text and listen to lecture.
EP	Test question: "List the five most influential psychologists of the twentieth century."

SEGMENT
Knowledge Dimension: Conceptual Knowledge
Cognitive Process: Apply

TG	Students will understand how the psychological theories of the twentieth century apply to current personal problems.
LO	Students completing this course will be able to apply concepts of twentieth-century psychology to current personal problems.
LE	Students will complete an internship at a local community mental health center.
EP	15-page research paper: "Select three types of personal psychological problems you worked with at your internship agency. Describe them in detail. Apply at least five perspectives of twentieth-century psychologists to each problem. Describe each perspective and how they differ in analysis of each problem."

or

EP	1-page report based on experience at community health center applying psychological concepts to profiles of three patients.

Figure 18.1   Example Course Blueprint Segments

CHAPTER 19

Building in Feedback

Classroom Assessment Techniques

LEARNING OBJECTIVES

Readers of this chapter will be able to:

- Describe the use of Classroom Assessment Techniques.
- Describe three types of Classroom Assessment Techniques.
- Describe three areas where Classroom Assessment Techniques can be used.

USING CLASSROOM ASSESSMENT TECHNIQUES (CATS) (Angelo & Cross, 1993) is one of the best ways for instructors to develop their ability to move beyond survival concerns to student learning. As opposed to end-of-term student evaluations, CATs provide real-time feedback to the instructor and students on how the course is going. The "central purpose of Classroom Assessment is to empower both teachers and their students to improve the quality of learning in the classroom" (Angelo & Cross, 1993, p. 4). CATs are

- Learner centered: "To improve learning, it may often be more effective to help students change their study habits or develop their metacognitive skills . . . than to change the instructor's teaching behavior" (p. 4).
- Teacher directed: "Classroom Assessment respects the autonomy, academic freedom, and professional judgment of college faculty. . . . The individual teacher decides what to assess, how to assess, and how to respond to the information gained through the assessment. Furthermore, the teacher is not obliged to share the results of Classroom Assessment with anyone outside the classroom" (p. 4).

- Mutually beneficial: "By cooperating in assessment, students reinforce their grasp of the course content and strengthen their own skills at self-assessment. Their motivation is increased when they realize that faculty are interested and invested in their success as learners. When students focus more clearly, participate more actively, and feel more confident that they can succeed, they are likely to do better in their course work" (pp. 4–5).
- Formative: "Classroom Assessments . . . are almost never graded and are almost always anonymous. Their aim is to provide faculty with information on what, how much, and how well students are learning, in order to help them better prepare to succeed—both on the subsequent graded evaluations and in the world beyond the classroom" (p. 5).
- Context specific: "To be most useful, Classroom Assessments have to respond to the particular needs and characteristics of the teachers, students, and disciplines to which they are applied. . . . As students interact in the classroom, the mixture of variables that can affect learning becomes vastly more complex. . . . As a result of these complex interactions, each

class develops its own 'microculture.' Classroom Assessment respects and depends on the faculty's professional judgment. . . ." (pp. 5–6).

- Ongoing: "Classroom Assessment is an ongoing process, perhaps best thought of as the creation and maintenance of a classroom 'feedback loop.' By employing a number of simple Classroom Assessment Techniques that are quick and easy to use, teachers get feedback from students on their learning. Faculty then complete the loop by providing students with feedback on the results of the assessment and suggestions for improving learning. . . . As this approach becomes integrated into everyday classroom activities, the communications loop connecting faculty to students—and teaching to learning—becomes more efficient and more effective" (p. 6).

- Rooted in good teaching practice: "Classroom Assessment provides a way to integrate assessment systematically and seamlessly into the traditional classroom teaching and learning process. . . . Directed practice in self-assessment . . . gives students the opportunity to develop metacognitive skills; that is, to become skilled in thinking carefully about their own thinking and learning" (p. 6).

CATs can be used to assess content, classroom process, and classroom culture and atmosphere. Figure 19.1 shows a grid of examples of three popular CATs designed to assess each category. "Minute Papers" are the most popularly used CAT and the most-used question in Minute Papers is, "What was the most important concept covered in class today?" sometimes with a "Muddiest Point" question on "What is still confusing to you?" Minute papers take 5 to 10 minutes for students to complete and can be given at any time during the class session: at the beginning, to see where everyone's thoughts are; in the middle, to begin or end a particular topic; or at the end, to survey the class session. "Categorizing grids" ask students to classify information by whatever categories are relevant to the subject. "Background knowledge probes" provide specific information that helps in selecting topics and designing learning experiences.

How does the use of CATs help instructors move beyond their focus on teaching survival skills? New instructors initially are not enthusiastic about having to

interact so directly with their students, but they quickly find that breaking down the instructor-student barrier is not only useful but enjoyable. Students in my "Teaching and Learning" course at the University of Pittsburgh reported

As a first-time teaching fellow, I was not looking forward, really, to doing a CAT and being criticized by the students early in the semester. However, I found it to be a great experience. It gave me an excellent opportunity to talk to my students on a more personal level. My class was an introductory one in my department and included a wide variety of student and experience levels. Many of the comments on the CATs were on the topic of the speed of the class; some thought it was going too slow, some too fast. So it gave me the chance to tell them about the diversity of the class.

I found the use of CATs to be valuable not only to my understanding of my students, but, surprisingly, noticed the CATs themselves had a positive effect on student attitudes. . . . . Although their responses helped me modify my style in an attempt to be more effective vis-à-vis their learning, I also found that students appreciated the effort on my part. I could see it in their expressions and heard it in their comments as we discussed the CAT in the lecture following its completion. . . . It seemed the class lightened up a bit from that point forward. . . . I was pleasantly surprised that subsequent discussions following the CATs were both productive and positive experiences for my students.

Research on the impact of CATs on students' perceptions of learning (Fabry, Eisenbach, Curry, & Golich, 1997) identified two major themes: increased student learning of the material and improved student feelings about the learning process. Students reported that CATs clarified and increased their understanding of the material, provided awareness and reflection, kept the class focused on goal achievement, gave accountability for self/peers, and provided proof of learning and new perspectives. Students felt better about the learning process because they felt CATs gave them a voice in the class, made them more self-confident and enthusiastic about learning, and improved their communication with the instructor.

Using the College and University Classroom Environment Inventory (CUCEI) (Treagust & Fraser, 1986),

Type → Purpose ↓	Minute Paper	Categorizing Grid	Background Knowledge Probe
Classroom culture and atmosphere	What question would you have liked to ask in class today? Why didn't you ask it?	Which topics are you worried or uncomfortable about discussing in class? | Comfortable | Uncomfortable | | | | 1. women's rights 2. gun control 3. school integration 4. homosexuality	What have been your experiences in courses covering sensitive subjects? 1 = yes 2 = no __ students respectful __ students aware of other points of view __ comfortable with discussion
Classroom process	Describe your favorite ways of learning (e.g., field trips, library, debates, research papers).	Which teaching and learning techniques are helpful to you? | Helpful | Not Helpful | | | | 1. lecture 2. discussion 3. small groups 4. research projects 5. debate 6. field trips	What teaching and learning techniques have you used in your courses? L = used a lot S = used some N = never used __ research paper __ small groups __ library project __ debates __ field trips
Content	What was the most important concept covered in class today?	This economic policy will affect which side of the economy? | Demand Side | Supply Side | | | | 1. reduction of federal income tax 2. airline deregulation 3. subsidized job training	Mark titles of plays you have encountered. R = read play T = saw on TV P = saw in theater W = worked on production __ *As You Like It* __ *Oklahoma* __ *Hamlet* __ *Showboat*

Figure 19.1   Examples of Three Types of CATs for Three Purposes

Kalina and Catlin (1994) found several significant differences between classes that regularly used CATs and those that did not use them at all: Retention in courses using CATs was increased from 1% to 8%; students in CAT classes received more A grades and fewer D and F grades; CAT classes were completed by 9% more females; ethnically diverse students had higher task understanding, cohesiveness, and personalization (CUCEI categories) in classes with CATs; and students reported more class involvement, cohesiveness, personalization, satisfaction, task understanding, and instructor innovation in CAT classes.

CHAPTER 20

Tests and Blueprints

LEARNING OBJECTIVES

Readers of this chapter will be able to:

- Design test questions for course content at the appropriate Bloom cognitive level.
- Use the Test Design Blueprint to analyze test results.

IT IS IMPORTANT TO DEVELOP TESTS THAT MATCH YOUR learning objectives as accurately as possible. A Test Design Blueprint (TDB) provides a structure for design so that you can relate each test item to the course objectives. Some courses will involve very few Blueprint cells, whereas others will include many different levels of cognition. Naturally, the more advanced levels will require that you verify your students have completed objectives at lower developmental levels.

A TDB should be constructed to be certain that each unit of content is evaluated at all applicable cognitive levels. The percentage of a test on any one content area should reflect the importance of the content, which usually corresponds to the amount of time spent on it in class. Objective tests can address a variety of cognitive levels and cover more topics than an essay. When you construct your exam, for each area of content include several questions from levels preceding your highest level so that you can identify the level of any errors. Questions can ask students to predict an outcome or apply concepts to given situations. Use the verbs from each of the taxonomy levels that match the verbs in your learning objectives. To measure "remember," use questions asking students to recognize, identify, recall, list, or retrieve. For "understand," have students illustrate, distinguish, categorize, compare, or map. To mea-

sure "apply," ask students to solve a problem, such as calculate a mathematical problem or apply a concept to a particular case. For "analyze," ask students questions that require them to distinguish between items, select appropriate evidence, or integrate elements. For "evaluate," ask questions that require they critique criteria and judge methods. And, to measure "create," ask students to compose, design, or construct. Figure 20.1 provides a sample TDB for two different content units in a course on U.S. history after 1918.

An important value of the Test Blueprint is that, after you have scored the items, you can evaluate where students have problems with the material and which test questions need to be refined. Calculate the percentage of students who answered each question correctly. According to Jacobs and Chase (1992), difficult items are those that are answered correctly by 50% to 70% of the class. They also point out that lack of preparation is not the only reason that students can miss answers; it also could be that the item is poorly written or that the material is difficult. On your Blueprint, you would expect students to have more correct answers for items in the lower cognitive levels than in the higher ones. Use your test analysis to guide further consideration of the material in class and to develop additional learning experiences for your students.

COURSE: U.S. HISTORY AFTER 1918

CONTENT AREA: GREAT DEPRESSION

Question	Remember	Understand	Apply	Analyze	Evaluate	Create
What year did the Great Depression begin?	x					
Name the president(s) of the U.S. during the Great Depression.	x					
Which of the following was a cause of the Great Depression? A.. Teapot Dome Scandal B. Discovery of gold in Utah C. Stock speculation		x				
What political impact did the Great Depression have on presidential politics in the U.S.?				x		

CONTENT AREA: SECOND WORLD WAR

Question	Remember	Understand	Apply	Analyze	Evaluate	Create
On what date did the U.S. enter WWII?	x					
Name the commander of the Allied Forces in 1943.	x					
In what year did the Germans surrender at Stalingrad in the first big defeat of Hitler's armies?	x					
Which of the following was a cause of WWII? A. Japan's need for raw materials B. Italy's pacifist government C. Germany's poor road system		x				
What political impact did WWII have on presidential politics in the U.S.?			x			
What were the economic results in the U.S. of entering WWII?				x		
After declaring the end to "the war to end all wars," what happened that resulted in Western leaders allowing another conflict to threaten their countries?					x	
How could WWII have been avoided?						x

Figure 20.1   Sample Test Design Blueprint

Note. The percentage of questions on each content area should reflect its importance in the unit.

Essay questions are included on your Blueprint and also require a rubric, which will be covered in the following chapter. Rubrics are explained and given to the students as they prepare for the test. Essays should not be used if the same material could be assessed through a multiple-choice test. Unruh (1988) suggests that the appropriate, higher-level tasks for essays are as follows:

- Comparing (identify similarities)
- Relating cause and effect (what are major causes?)

- Justifying (why you agree)
- Generalizing (drawing a set of principles)
- Inferring (how would a character react to a situation?)
- Creating (what would happen if . . . ?)

Jacobs and Chase (1992) recommend having students write several shorter essays rather than giving them a choice of which questions to write on a longer one. In a 50-minute class session, students can answer 3 essay questions or 10 short-answer questions.

When grading essays, read and grade each question across tests, rather than grade all of one student's test. Take a quick look at all of the exams before you start grading. Write brief notes on the student papers and provide the scored rubric with the grade so that students will be able to identify their weaknesses and strengths. If possible, read only a few essays at a time and read each essay twice. You will be able to evaluate the test with the Blueprint and by analyzing scores on the different elements on the essay rubric.

CHAPTER 21

Assignments and Rubrics

LEARNING OBJECTIVES

Readers of this chapter will be able to:

- Design learning experiences for students to use to achieve learning objectives.
- Design rubrics to specify criteria for levels of ability for meeting learning objectives.

ASSIGNMENTS ARE LEARNING EXPERIENCES THAT PROvide students the chance to practice their skills and to receive feedback on their accomplishments. Sometimes the feedback is for development and other times for grading. Assignments, like tests, need to fall into the same Blueprint cell as their teaching goals and learning objectives. According to Morrison and Ross (1998), more and more assignments are "open-ended learning environments, such as problem-based learning, which provide a different type of learning experience and product than is produced in the traditional learning environment. . . . The learning resulting from such an approach is not easily assessed with a traditional paper-and-pencil test but requires evaluation that is geared to the real world and grounded in performance standards" (p. 69).

Morrison and Ross (1998) go on to say that "using holistic scoring procedures or rubrics, for instance, potentially increases the reliability of assessing such complex performances and the richness of information provided to students regarding their level of achievement" (1998, pp. 69–70). Rubrics provide both criteria and standards for an assignment. Students often are not clear on what is expected. A rubric can be used to clarify assignments and to assess them. With a rubric, students are able to evaluate their own and their colleagues' work,

improving their assignments and saving the instructor time and effort. Rubrics are provided to students along with each assignment, although some rubrics will cover many similar assignments, such as essays or research papers. Although time-consuming to develop, rubrics make student work better and grading easier.

Clear rubrics can be the basis for departmental discussions of course standards and be used to sequence courses. They can provide consistency in grading across course sections and provide evidence of learning to accrediting agencies.

Developing a rubric requires two steps: first, identifying the necessary elements of an assignment and, second, stating the criteria for achievement. The first rubric (Figure 21.1) was developed for oral reports. Elements to be evaluated are focus on topic, content, enthusiasm, posture and eye contact, presentation activities and/or technology, generalizability, time limit, and clear speech. A short description is provided for different levels of achievement for each element. For instance, focus on topic can be rated from 0, for "hard to tell what the topic was," to 3, for "stays on topic all of the time." This may seem obvious when it has been stated, but developing the criteria for each element is difficult and takes time. The second rubric (Figure 21.2) was provided by Bean and Peterson (1998) to

CATEGORY	3	2	1	0
Focus on Topic	Stays on topic all of the time	Stays on topic most of the time	Stays on topic some of the time	Was hard to tell what the topic was
Content	Shows a full understanding of the topic	Shows a good understanding of the topic	Shows some understanding of the topic	Does not seem to understand the topic very well
Enthusiasm	Facial expressions and body language generate a strong interest and enthusiasm about the topic in others	Facial expressions and body language sometimes generate a strong interest and enthusiasm about the topic	Facial expressions and body language are used to try to generate enthusiasm, but seem somewhat faked	Very little use of facial expressions or body language. Did not generate much interest in topic being presented
Posture and Eye Contact	Stands up straight, looks relaxed and confident. Establishes eye contact with everyone in the room during the presentation	Stands up straight and establishes eye contact with several people in the room during the presentation	Sometimes stands up straight and establishes eye contact	Slouches and/or does not look at people during the presentation
Presentation Activities and/or Technology	Adequately used and significantly contributed to audience learning	Adequately used and moderately effective in contributing to audience learning	Adequately used but not effective in contributing to audience learning	Minimal to no use of presentation activities and/or technology
Generalizability	Applicable to a broad range of courses and topics	Applicable only within the presenter's department	Applicable only within presenter's department	Applicable only to presenter's course
Time Limit	Presentation is 10–20 minutes	Presentation is 7–9 minutes	Presentation is 5–6 minutes	Presentation is less than 5 minutes OR more than 20 minutes
Clear Speech	Speaks clearly and distinctly all of the time	Speaks clearly and distinctly most of the time	Speaks clearly and distinctly some of the time	Often mumbles or cannot be understood

Figure 21.1   Oral Presentation Rubric

grade class participation. They have operationalized their expectations and, as can be seen from the notes, have modified it with student feedback.

An excellent resource for beginning the development of rubrics can be found at http://rubistar.4teachers .org/index.php. RubiStar provides sample rubrics posted by teachers and faculty members on topics as wide ranging as chemistry research projects and proper behavior at classical music concerts. There is no charge for viewing and using the RubiStar rubrics, and usually a category is already begun for almost any assignment. Rubrics also are provided in *Effective Grading: A Tool for Learning and Assessment* (1998) by Walvoord and Anderson, in *Assessing Student Learning: A Common Sense Guide* (Suskie, 2004), and in *Changing the Way We Grade Student Performance: Classroom Assessment and the New Learning Paradigm* (Anderson & Speck, 1998).

Holistic Rubric for Scoring Class Participation

6	A student receiving a 6 comes to class prepared,[1] contributes readily to the conversation, but doesn't dominate it; makes thoughtful contributions that advance the conversation; shows interest in and respect for others' views; participates actively in small groups.
5	Comes to class prepared and makes thoughtful comments when called upon; contributes occasionally without prompting; shows interest in and respect for others' views; participates actively in small groups. A 5 score may also be appropriate to an active participant whose contributions are less developed or cogent than those of a 6, but still advance the conversation.
4	A student receiving a 4 participates in discussion, but in a problematic way. Such students may talk too much, make rambling or tangential contributions, continually interrupt the instructor with digressive questions, bluff their way when unprepared, or otherwise dominate discussions, not acknowledging cues of annoyance from instructor or students. Students in this category often profit from a conference with the instructor.
3	A student receiving a 3 comes to class prepared, but does not voluntarily contribute to discussions and gives only minimal answers when called upon. Nevertheless, these students show interest in the discussion, listen attentively, and take notes. Students in this category may be shy or introverted. The instructor may choose to give such students a 5 if they participate fully in small group discussions. Sympathetic counseling of such students often helps.[2]
2–1	Students in this range often seem on the margins of the class and may have a negative effect on the participation of others. Students receiving a 2 often don't participate because they haven't read the material or done the homework. Students receiving a 1 may be actually disruptive, radiating negative energy via hostile or bored body language, or be overtly rude.

Figure 21.2 Class Participation Rubric

Note: This scoring guide assumes regular attendance; the instructor may lower participation scores for absences or tardiness.
[1]Preparation can be measured by quizzes, by brief writing assignments at the start of class, by completion of out-of-class journal entries or other homework, or by evidence from direct questioning.

[2]During class discussions of this rubric, we have found that students often want to reverse the 4's and the 3's. They will argue that a quiet student who actively listens deserves more points than the dominating/annoying student. Teachers may wish to follow this suggestion.

Note. From "Grading Classroom Participation," by J. C. Bean and D. Peterson, 1998, in R. S. Anderson and B. W. Speck (Eds.), *Changing the Way We Grade Student Performance: Classroom Assessment and the New Learning Paradigm* (p. 36). New Directions for Teaching and Learning, No. 74. San Francisco: Jossey-Bass. Copyright 1998 by Jossey-Bass. Reprinted with permission.

SECTION FOUR

Documenting Learning

THE "TEACHING" PORTFOLIO WAS DEVELOPED IN THE EARLY 1970S AT North American colleges and universities to supplement the use of student evaluations. By assembling a wide range of teaching materials, it was believed that instructors would be better able to demonstrate, and administrators better able to evaluate, teaching effectiveness than by the single measure of student satisfaction. Christopher Knapper (1995) described in his article "The Origins of Teaching Portfolios" the process by which the "dossier" was developed by a committee of the Canadian Association of University Teachers that he chaired. The committee recommended including in a portfolio three types of "evidence":

1. Products of good teaching, such as student work
2. Materials from oneself, such as syllabi
3. Information from others, such as student ratings

The use of portfolios has spread to instructors at universities around the world, with many different designs. One of the original "teaching" portfolio designs in the United States was used first at the University of Pittsburgh in the early 1980s and adapted by Richlin and Manning (1995) to include five sections:

1. Description of teaching responsibilities
2. Teaching philosophy
3. Representative instructional materials
   a. Syllabus with commentary
   b. Assignments with commentary
   c. Student work with instructor's feedback and commentary

4. Evaluations of teaching from students, peers, and others
5. Professional development plan

As Brenda Manning and I worked with hundreds of faculty members to document their teaching activities, it became obvious that a "teaching" portfolio made little sense because it had parts from so many different courses and times. Cerbin (1994) initiated the change to focusing on individual courses by creating "course" portfolios, which provides a more cohesive process because all materials refer to a specific set of objectives. The main benefit of the course portfolio is the ease it affords an instructor for tracing the connections among learning objectives, learning experiences, and student achievement.

This section describes a useful blueprint for a course design portfolio that focuses on how you conceptualize and operationalize student learning in one particular course. You can use a course design portfolio in at least three ways. The most important, of course, is for redesign when you reconsider your goals, student objectives, and learning activities for future courses. The second purpose is for documentation of your teaching effectiveness to present for hiring, promotion, and tenure, as well as for departmental curriculum development and accreditation. The third purpose is for sharing your methods and results with your colleagues as a form of the Scholarship of Teaching and Learning.

The portfolio includes three sections: the course syllabus, attachments, and an explanation of each of the design decisions that resulted in how you created the syllabus and attachments. Figure A provides a listing of all course portfolio elements. Section 5 provides resources and planning instruments for the elements.

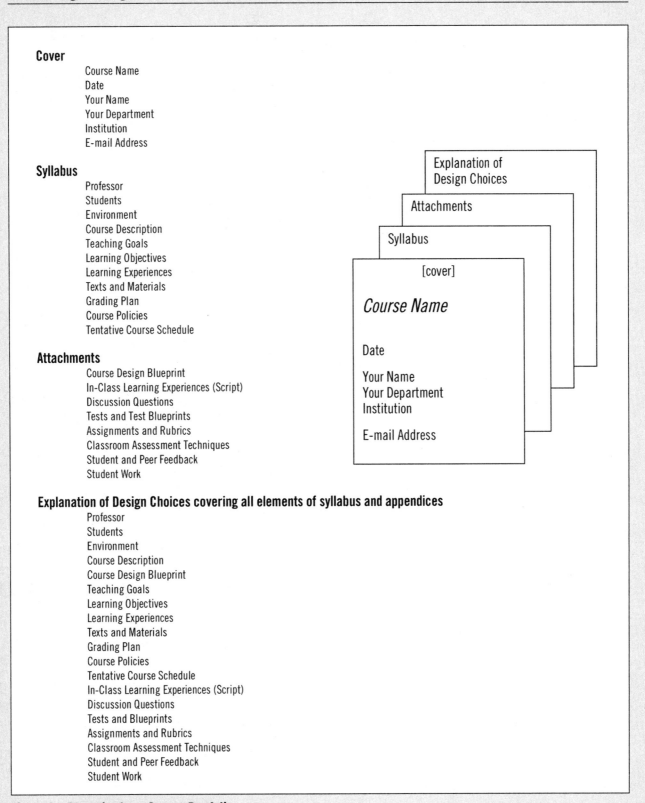

Cover
> Course Name
> Date
> Your Name
> Your Department
> Institution
> E-mail Address

Syllabus
> Professor
> Students
> Environment
> Course Description
> Teaching Goals
> Learning Objectives
> Learning Experiences
> Texts and Materials
> Grading Plan
> Course Policies
> Tentative Course Schedule

Attachments
> Course Design Blueprint
> In-Class Learning Experiences (Script)
> Discussion Questions
> Tests and Test Blueprints
> Assignments and Rubrics
> Classroom Assessment Techniques
> Student and Peer Feedback
> Student Work

Explanation of Design Choices covering all elements of syllabus and appendices
> Professor
> Students
> Environment
> Course Description
> Course Design Blueprint
> Teaching Goals
> Learning Objectives
> Learning Experiences
> Texts and Materials
> Grading Plan
> Course Policies
> Tentative Course Schedule
> In-Class Learning Experiences (Script)
> Discussion Questions
> Tests and Blueprints
> Assignments and Rubrics
> Classroom Assessment Techniques
> Student and Peer Feedback
> Student Work

Figure A   Blueprint for a Course Portfolio

CHAPTER 22

Syllabus

LEARNING OBJECTIVES

Readers of this chapter will be able to:

- Describe the elements of a scholarly syllabus.
- Assemble their TGs, LOs, LEs, and EPs into a scholarly syllabus for their course.

A VARIETY OF FORMATS ARE USED BY DISCIPLINES, DE-partments, and institutions for their syllabi. Some syllabi, particularly in the sciences, are very short, whereas others, particularly in the humanities, are much longer. A syllabus that is too short can frustrate students who need to plan ahead for the course requirements, activities, and schedule. Too long a syllabus can intimidate students by overwhelming them with details they will not need until the course is under way. A useful alternative is to provide a moderate length (four- to five-page) syllabus with "hooks" for attachments to be provided later. For instance, a common hook is to specify that details on a research project will be distributed at the third meeting of the course. This way the additional material becomes part of the official syllabus but leaves the basic syllabus focused on the most important points.

As we discussed in section 1, the first consideration in designing and documenting a course is the professor. How (phone, e-mail, in person), when (office hours, online response time), and where (office, home, pub) can you be contacted? What should your students know about you to aid them in learning in this course? This is the place to introduce yourself, providing information about your own education and research, and relating your interests and background to the course material.

This also is the place to describe the type of students for whom the course is designed. Is it a general education course, open to all majors? Are there prerequisites, either previous courses or skills necessary, for students to complete before they can learn the material?

The next consideration is the environment. When and where will the course meet? What equipment will be available? Are the students expected to bring—or are not allowed to use—notebook computers (or graphing calculators or their own paintbrushes) in class? Is the classroom equipped with Internet access? Will laboratory storage be provided?

A well-written course description will motivate students (and remind instructors why they are teaching) because it connects the work in the course to the important questions of the discipline and the day. This is where to describe your hopes and dreams for your students' relationship to this material. What is exciting about this topic? What are the big questions that the course will answer? What is the place of this course in the curriculum of the college? The department? The major? The discipline? What current problems or interests will this course enable your students to investigate?

Next it's time to consider what goals you have for

teaching this course. What will your students actually know and be able to do after completing this course? Describe what students can expect and be expected to do in class meetings, such as listening to lectures, working in groups, and making presentations. Describe outside-of-class meetings, including study groups, service learning, and attendance at events.

The fifth step is to list texts and materials. Require only texts and materials that you will use in the course. Explain where to purchase unusual items and any additional costs the students will be required to pay for materials you will supply. Be respectful of student budgets. Use proper citation format to set a good example for your students on how they are to cite references.

Next, explain the grading plan, including points and percentages for each test and assignment and the distribution of letter grades for points and percentages. Include policies for late papers, missed tests, attendance, academic honesty, and any departmental or institutional policies that apply.

Finally, list dates, in-class activities, and preparation required, such as text to read and assignments due. Be sure to label the plans as a "tentative" schedule and reserve the right to make adjustments as circumstances require.

CHAPTER 23

Attachments

LEARNING OBJECTIVES

Readers of this chapter will be able to:

- Provide materials demonstrating multiple aspects of the course design.
- Demonstrate the integration of course elements.

THE MOST SIGNIFICANT ATTACHMENT INCLUDED IN the course portfolio is the Course Design Blueprint detailing the teaching goals, learning objectives, learning experiences, and evaluation plans for the course. The Blueprint provides the overall direction for the course.

Attachments are able to provide the details of what takes place during the course. For instance, the in-class learning experience script, designed by Grasha (see Figure 10.6), demonstrates the variety of activities that take place in a class session, the amount of time spent on each unit of content, the materials and audiovisual technology required, along with a diversity check to specify students with which types of learning styles are most likely to learn from each activity.

Another useful attachment in your course portfolio is a selection of Playground, Brainstorm, and Focal questions for use in course discussions, in Classroom Assessment Techniques, and on quizzes and tests. Each

quiz and test also should be included with an accompanying test Blueprint indicating the content and Bloom level of each question so that the assessment can be correlated with the LOs, and so that the test results can be analyzed for consistent problems in student learning. Assignments, along with their rubrics, are other important attachments in the portfolio. Both the Blueprints and rubrics demonstrate the scholarly criteria used by the instructor in the assessment process.

The course portfolio also should include student and peer feedback from this course taught in the past. Summarize each instance of feedback by demonstrated strengths and weaknesses and discuss plans for addressing the challenges. In addition, include excellent, good, and poor samples of student work from previous times you have taught this course, along with the scored rubrics and the comments/feedback provided to your students.

CHAPTER 24

Explanation of Design Choices

LEARNING OBJECTIVES

Readers of this chapter will be able to:

- Describe the design choices made for the course.
- Justify design choices based on course specifics.
- Justify design choices based on learning theories.

AN ESSENTIAL PART OF A COURSE PORTFOLIO IS AN EX-planation of the course design. This will explain your choices to others, as well as remind you why and how you created the course goals, activities, and assessment, so that you can make necessary adjustments the next time you teach the course. The following suggestions and questions are designed to help focus the explanation:

- *Professor:* Describe how characteristics about you, such as your age, education, learning and teaching styles, experience, and other responsibilities, will (or will not) influence how you design the course.
- *Students:* Describe the students in terms of learning styles and other characteristics that influence their learning.
- *Environment:* Explain how the environment influenced how you designed the course. What opportunities or restrictions will there be based on when and where the course meets?
- *Course Description:* What are your hopes and dreams for your students in this course? Why is this material exciting? What areas did you not include? Why? How do students best learn this material? How will your teaching in this

course help meet your goals? Put the course into context.

- *Course Design Blueprint:* Discuss how you chose the content and set the Bloom levels for each teaching goal (TG) and learning objective (LO).
- *Teaching Goals:* Translate your hopes and dreams into your goals for teaching this course. Describe why these are the most important goals.
- *Learning Objectives:* Describe why these are the most important objectives for your students to achieve. What will your students actually know and be able to do after completing this course?
- *Learning Experiences:* Explain how these experiences will assist students in meeting LOs.
- *Texts and Materials:* Explain why you chose the texts and materials you did, including how they match the requirements and levels of the LOs.
- *In-Class Learning Experience Script:* Explain why you chose these experiences to meet your TGs and LOs, how you decided on the amount of time spent on each area of content, and how you have alternated activities to meet the learning needs of different types of students.

- *Discussion Questions:* Explain choices of structure, content, and developmental level for your questions.

- *Tests and Test Blueprints:* Explain how you determined the levels of questions in the Test Blueprints for all objective tests, including the learning objectives and material covered, and how you allocated points or questions. If you use other types of evaluation situations, describe the Blueprints and explanations for them.

- *Assignments and Rubrics:* Explain why you chose the assignments, why you selected the quality indicators for the rubrics you developed, and the opportunities your students will have to practice and receive feedback without assessment. If you plan to grade in-class efforts ("participation"), be sure to provide a rubric describing exactly what you expect students to do.

- *Classroom Assessment Techniques (CATs):* Explain why you created the CATs to provide you with feedback on classroom content, process, and ambiance. If you have used the CATs before, provide your analysis of the responses.

- *Student and Peer Feedback:* Describe your reaction and whether or not you agree with the feedback you received. Describe your efforts or intentions to address any weaknesses and to continue the strengths.

- *Student Work:* Describe the samples in terms of your teaching goals and course learning objectives. Describe the variety of evaluation situations of the samples and why you chose them. Explain how you decided on the Blueprints for each example, including the LOs and material covered, how you allocated points, and the level of cognition required.

SECTION FIVE

Learning Resources and Planning Instruments

THE INFORMATION IN THIS SECTION PROVIDES ADDITIONAL BACKGROUND and inventories for you to use in designing your course.

Seven Principles for Good Practice in Undergraduate Education

The group assembled to create the Seven Principles was composed of Alexander W. Austin (UCLA), Howard Bowen (Claremont Colleges), William Boyd (Johnson Foundation), Carol M. Boyer (Education Commission of the States), K. Patricia Cross (Harvard), Kenneth Eble (University of Utah), Russell Edgerton (American Association for Higher Education), Jerry Gaff (Hamline University), Henry Halsted (Johnson Foundation), Joseph Katz (State University of New York at Stony Brook), C. Robert Pace (UCLA), Marvin Peterson (University of Michigan), and Richard C. Richardson, Jr. (Arizona State University). The two-day conference was co-sponsored by the Johnson Foundation, American Association for Higher Education (AAHE), and the Education Commission of the States.

1. **Good Practice Encourages Student-Faculty Contact.** Frequent student-faculty contact in and out of classes is the most important factor in student motivation and involvement. Faculty concern helps students get through rough times and keep on working. Knowing a few faculty members well enhances students' intellectual commitment and encourages them to think about their own values and future plans.

2. **Good Practice Encourages Cooperation Among Students.** Learning is enhanced when it is more like a team effort than a solo race. Good learning, like good work, is collaborative and social, not competitive and isolated. Working with others often increases involvement in learning. Sharing one's own ideas and responding to others' reactions improves thinking and deepens understanding.

3. **Good Practice Encourages Active Learning.** Learning is not a spectator sport. Students do not learn much just sitting in classes listening to teachers, memorizing pre-packaged assignments, and spitting out answers. They must talk about what they are learning, write about it, re-

late it to past experiences, and apply it to their daily lives.

4. **Good Practice Gives Prompt Feedback.** Knowing what you know and don't know focuses learning. Students need appropriate feedback on performance to benefit from courses. In getting started, students need help in assessing existing knowledge and competence. In classes, students need frequent opportunities to perform and receive suggestions for improvement. At various points during college, and at the end, students need chances to reflect on what they have learned, what they still need to know, and how to assess themselves.

5. **Good Practice Emphasizes Time on Task.** Time plus energy equals learning. There is no substitute for time on task. Learning to use one's time well is critical for students and professionals alike. Students need help in learning effective time management. Allocating realistic amounts of time means effective learning for students and effective teaching for faculty. How an institution defines time expectations for students, faculty, administrators,

and other professional staff can establish the basis for high performance for all.

6. **Good Practice Communicates High Expectations.** Expect more and you will get it. High expectations are important for everyone—for the poorly prepared, for those unwilling to expect themselves, and for the bright and well motivated. Expecting students to perform well becomes a self-fulfilling prophecy when teachers and institutions hold high expectations for themselves and make extra efforts.

7. **Good Practice Respects Diverse Talents and Ways of Learning.** There are many roads to learning. People bring different talents and styles of learning to college. Brilliant students in the seminar room may be all thumbs in the lab or art studio. Students rich in hands-on experience may not do well with theory. Students need the opportunity to show their talents and learn in ways that work for them. Then they can be pushed to learning in new ways that do not come so easily.

Learner-Centered Psychological Principles

The following 14 psychological principles pertain to the learner and the learning process.* They focus on psychological factors that are primarily internal to and under the control of the learner rather than conditioned habits or physiological factors. However, the principles also attempt to acknowledge external environment or contextual factors that interact with these internal factors. The principles are intended to deal holistically with learners in the context of real-world learning situations. Thus, they are best understood as an organized set of principles; no principle should be viewed in isolation. Principles are intended to apply to all learners—from children, to teachers, to administrators, to parents, and to community members involved in our educational system.

Cognitive and Metacognitive Factors

1. **Nature of the learning process.**
   The learning of complex subject matter is most effective when it is an intentional process of constructing meaning from information and experience.
   There are different types of learning processes, for example, habit formation in motor learning; and learning that involves the generation of knowledge, or cognitive skills and learning strategies. Learning in schools emphasizes the use of intentional processes that students can use to construct meaning from information, experiences, and their own thoughts and beliefs. Successful learners are active, goal-directed, self-regulating, and assume personal responsibility for contributing to their own learning. The principles set forth in this document focus on this type of learning.

2. **Goals of the learning process.**
   The successful learner, over time and with support and instructional guidance, can create meaningful, coherent representations of knowledge.
   The strategic nature of learning requires students to be goal directed. To construct useful representations of knowledge and to acquire the thinking and learning strategies necessary for continued learning success across the life span, students must generate and pursue personally relevant goals. Initially, students' short-term goals and learning may be sketchy in an area, but over time their understanding can be refined by filling gaps, resolving inconsistencies, and deepening their understanding of the subject matter so that they can reach longer-term goals. Educators can assist learners in creating meaningful learning goals that are consistent with both personal and educational aspirations and interests.

---

* The development of each principle involved thorough discussions of the research supporting that principle. The multidisciplinary research expertise of the Task Force and Work Group members facilitated an examination of each principle from a number of different research perspectives.

3. **Construction of knowledge.**

   The successful learner can link new information with existing knowledge in meaningful ways.

   Knowledge widens and deepens as students continue to build links between new information and experiences and their existing knowledge base. The nature of these links can take a variety of forms, such as adding to, modifying, or reorganizing existing knowledge or skills. How these links are made or develop may vary in different subject areas, and among students with varying talents, interests, and abilities. However, unless new knowledge becomes integrated with the learner's prior knowledge and understanding, this new knowledge remains isolated, cannot be used most effectively in new tasks, and does not transfer readily to new situations. Educators can assist learners in acquiring and integrating knowledge by a number of strategies that have been shown to be effective with learners of varying abilities, such as concept mapping and thematic organization or categorizing.

4. **Strategic thinking.**

   The successful learner can create and use a repertoire of thinking and reasoning strategies to achieve complex learning goals.

   Successful learners use strategic thinking in their approach to learning, reasoning, problem solving, and concept learning. They understand and can use a variety of strategies to help them reach learning and performance goals, and to apply their knowledge in novel situations. They also continue to expand their repertoire of strategies by reflecting on the methods they use to see which work well for them, by receiving guided instruction and feedback, and by observing or interacting with appropriate models. Learning outcomes can be enhanced if educators assist learners in developing, applying, and assessing their strategic learning skills.

5. **Thinking about thinking.**

   Higher order strategies for selecting and monitoring mental operations facilitate creative and critical thinking.

   Successful learners can reflect on how they think and learn, set reasonable learning or performance goals, select potentially appropriate learning strategies or methods, and monitor their progress toward these goals. In addition, successful learners know what to do if a problem occurs or if they are not making sufficient or timely progress toward a goal. They can generate alternative methods to reach their goal (or reassess the appropriateness and utility of the goal). Instructional methods that focus on helping learners develop these higher order (metacognitive) strategies can enhance student learning and personal responsibility for learning.

6. **Context of learning.**

   Learning is influenced by environmental factors, including culture, technology, and instructional practices.

   Learning does not occur in a vacuum. Teachers play a major interactive role with both the learner and the learning environment. Cultural or group influences on students can impact many educationally relevant variables, such as motivation, orientation toward learning, and ways of thinking. Technologies and instructional practices must be appropriate for learners' level of prior knowledge, cognitive abilities, and their learning and thinking strategies. The classroom environment, particularly the degree to which it is nurturing or not, can also have significant impacts on student learning.

Motivational and Affective Factors

7. **Motivational and emotional influences on learning.**

   What and how much is learned is influenced by the motivation. Motivation to learn, in turn, is influenced by the individual's emotional states, beliefs, interests and goals, and habits of thinking.

   The rich internal world of thoughts, beliefs, goals, and expectations for success or failure can enhance or interfere with the learner's quality of thinking and information processing. Students' beliefs about themselves as learners and the nature of learning have a marked influence on motivation. Motivational and emotional factors also influence both the quality of thinking and information processing as well as an individual's motivation to learn. Positive emotions, such as curiosity, generally enhance motivation and facilitate learning and performance. Mild anxiety can also enhance learning and performance by focusing the learner's attention on a particular task. However, intense negative emotions (e.g., anxiety, panic, rage, insecurity) and related thoughts (e.g., worrying about competence, ruminating about failure, fearing punishment, ridicule, or stigmatizing labels) generally detract from motivation, interfere with learning, and contribute to low performance.

8. **Intrinsic motivation to learn.**

The learner's creativity, higher order thinking, and natural curiosity all contribute to motivation to learn. Intrinsic motivation is stimulated by tasks of optimal novelty and difficulty, relevant to personal interests, and providing for personal choice and control.

Curiosity, flexible and insightful thinking, and creativity are major indicators of the learners' intrinsic motivation to learn, which is in large part a function of meeting basic needs to be competent and to exercise personal control. Intrinsic motivation is facilitated on tasks that learners perceive as interesting and personally relevant and meaningful, appropriate in complexity and difficulty to the learners' abilities, and on which they believe they can succeed. Intrinsic motivation is also facilitated on tasks that are comparable to real-world situations and meet needs for choice and control. Educators can encourage and support learners' natural curiosity and motivation to learn by attending to individual differences in learners' perceptions of optimal novelty and difficulty, relevance, and personal choice and control.

9. **Effects of motivation on effort.**

Acquisition of complex knowledge and skills requires extended learner effort and guided practice. Without learners' motivation to learn, the willingness to exert this effort is unlikely without coercion.

Effort is another major indicator of motivation to learn. The acquisition of complex knowledge and skills demands the investment of considerable learner energy and strategic effort, along with persistence over time. Educators need to be concerned with facilitating motivation by strategies that enhance learner effort and commitment to learning and to achieving high standards of comprehension and understanding. Effective strategies include purposeful learning activities, guided by practices that enhance positive emotions and intrinsic motivation to learn, and methods that increase learners' perceptions that a task is interesting and personally relevant.

Developmental and Social Factors

10. **Developmental influences on learning.**

As individuals develop, there are different opportunities and constraints for learning. Learning is most effective when differential development within and across physical, intellectual, emotional, and social domains is taken into account.

Individuals learn best when material is appropriate to their developmental level and is presented in an enjoyable and interesting way. Because individual development varies across intellectual, social, emotional, and physical domains, achievement in different instructional domains may also vary. Overemphasis on one type of developmental readiness—such as reading readiness, for example—may preclude learners from demonstrating that they are more capable in other areas of performance. The cognitive, emotional, and social development of individual learners and how they interpret life experiences are affected by prior schooling, home, culture, and community factors. Early and continuing parental involvement in schooling, and the quality of language interactions and two-way communications between adults and children can influence these developmental areas. Awareness and understanding of developmental differences among children with and without emotional, physical, or intellectual disabilities, can facilitate the creation of optimal learning contexts.

11. **Social influences on learning.**

Learning is influenced by social interactions, interpersonal relations, and communication with others.

Learning can be enhanced when the learner has an opportunity to interact and to collaborate with others on instructional tasks. Learning settings that allow for social interactions, and that respect diversity, encourage flexible thinking and social competence. In interactive and collaborative instructional contexts, individuals have an opportunity for perspective taking and reflective thinking that may lead to higher levels of cognitive, social, and moral development, as well as self-esteem. Quality personal relationships that provide stability, trust, and caring can increase learners' sense of belonging, self-respect and self-acceptance, and provide a positive climate for learning. Family influences, positive interpersonal support and instruction in self-motivation strategies can offset factors that interfere with optimal learning such as negative beliefs about competence in a particular subject, high levels of test anxiety, negative sex role expectations, and undue pressure to perform well. Positive learning climates can also help to establish the context for healthier levels of thinking, feeling, and behaving. Such contexts help learners feel safe to share ideas, actively participate in the learning process, and create a learning community.

Individual Differences Factors

12. **Individual differences in learning.**
Learners have different strategies, approaches, and capabilities for learning that are a function of prior experience and heredity.
Individuals are born with and develop their own capabilities and talents. In addition, through learning and social acculturation, they have acquired their own preferences for how they like to learn and the pace at which they learn. However, these preferences are not always useful in helping learners reach their learning goals. Educators need to help students examine their learning preferences and expand or modify them, if necessary. The interaction between learner differences and curricular and environmental conditions is another key factor affecting learning outcomes. Educators need to be sensitive to individual differences, in general. They also need to attend to learner perceptions of the degree to which these differences are accepted and adapted to by varying instructional methods and materials.

13. **Learning and diversity.**
Learning is most effective when differences in learners' linguistic, cultural, and social backgrounds are taken into account.
The same basic principles of learning, motivation, and effective instruction apply to all learners. However, language, ethnicity, race, beliefs, and socioeconomic status all can influence learning. Careful attention to these factors in the instruc-

tional setting enhances the possibilities for designing and implementing appropriate learning environments. When learners perceive that their individual differences in abilities, backgrounds, cultures, and experiences are valued, respected, and accommodated in learning tasks and contexts, levels of motivation and achievement are enhanced.

14. **Standards and assessment.**
Setting appropriately high and challenging standards and assessing the learner as well as learning progress—including diagnostic, process, and outcome assessment—are integral parts of the learning process.
Assessment provides important information to both the learner and teacher at all stages of the learning process. Effective learning takes place when learners feel challenged to work towards appropriately high goals; therefore, appraisal of the learner's cognitive strengths and weaknesses, as well as current knowledge and skills, is important for the selection of instructional materials of an optimal degree of difficulty. Ongoing assessment of the learner's understanding of the curricular material can provide valuable feedback to both learners and teachers about progress toward the learning goals. Standardized assessment of learner progress and outcomes assessment provides one type of information about achievement levels both within and across individuals that can inform various types of programmatic decisions. Performance assessments can provide other sources of information about the attainment of learning outcomes. Self-assessments of learning progress can also improve students' self appraisal skills and enhance motivation and self-directed learning.

Elements and Reflective Questions for Course Portfolio Design: Syllabus, Attachments, and Explanation

SYLLABUS AND DESIGN EXPLANATION

Syllabus Elements	Design Explanation
Professor Who is the instructor (who are you)? How (phone, e-mail, in person), when, and where can you be contacted?	*Professor* Describe how your age, education, learning styles, learning and teaching styles, experience, and other characteristics important to you, as well as your other responsibilities, will (or will not) influence how you design the course, including how available you plan to be to your students.
Students Describe your students in terms of learning styles and other characteristics that influence their learning.	*Students* How have the students you expect in the course influenced your course design? What characteristics were most important?
Environment What days and times will the course meet? Where will the course meet?	*Environment* Describe the influence of the environment on how you design the course. What opportunities or restrictions will there be based on when and where the course meets?
Course Description What are your hopes and dreams for your students' relationship to this topic? What is exciting about this topic? What are the big questions that this course will answer? For which students is the course designed? (e.g., level, major, interests) What is the place of this course in the curriculum of the college? The department? The major? The discipline?	*Course Description* What are your hopes and dreams for your students in this course? Why is this material exciting? What areas did you not include? Why? How do students best learn this material? How will your teaching in this course help meet your goals? Put the course into context.

Syllabus Elements	Design Explanation
Teaching Goals What goals do you have for teaching this course?	*Teaching Goals* Translate your hopes and dreams into your goals for teaching this course. Explain why these are the most important goals.
Learning Objectives What will your students actually know and be able to do after completing this course? "Students completing this course will be able to . . ."	*Learning Objectives* This is the most important step in the process of designing a course. Put your students' learning objectives in the format "Students completing this course will be able to . . ." and list them in advancing levels of cognitive difficulty for each unit. Explain why these are the most important objectives for your students to achieve.
Texts and Materials List texts and materials using proper format for your discipline. Explain where to purchase unusual items and any additional costs the students will be required to pay for materials you will supply.	*Texts and Materials* Explain why you chose the texts and materials you did, including how they match the requirements and levels of the learning objectives. Require only texts and materials that you will use in the course. Be respectful of student budgets. Use proper citation format to set a good example for your students on how they are to cite references.
Grading Plan Explain the grading plan, including points and percentages for each test and assignment and the distribution of letter grades for points and percentages.	*Grading Plan* Explain why you designed your grading plan. Be sure that all graded activities are directed at the learning objectives and that you are grading all learning objectives listed.
Learning Experiences Describe what students can expect and be expected to do in class meetings, such as listening to lectures, working in groups, and making presentations. Describe outside-of-class meetings, including study groups, service learning, and attendance at events.	*Learning Experiences* Explain how these experiences will assist students in meeting learning objectives.
Course Policies List your policies for late papers, missed tests, attendance, academic honesty, and any departmental or institutional policies that apply.	*Course Policies* Explain your policies in light of student learning in this course.
Tentative Course Schedule List dates, in-class activities, and preparation required, such as text to read and assignments due.	*Tentative Course Schedule* Explain why you have scheduled topics and activities in the order listed. Explain why you may need to change the schedule.

ATTACHMENTS AND DESIGN EXPLANATION

Attachment Elements	Design Explanation
In-Class Learning Experience (Script) Describe in detail a class session including time line, content, activities, diversity check, materials, and audiovisual technology required.	*In-Class Learning Experience (Script)* Explain why you have chosen these activities to meet your teaching goals and learning objectives.
Discussion Questions Create playground, brainstorm, and focal questions for use in your course.	*Discussion Questions* Explain choices of content and developmental level for questions.
Tests and Test Blueprints Create and describe in detail tests and provide blueprints for each test.	*Tests and Test Blueprints* Explain how you determined the test blueprints for all objective tests, including the learning objectives and material covered, how you allocated points or questions, and the level of cognition required.
Other Types of Evaluation Situations and Blueprints Create and describe in detail other types of evaluation situations and provide blueprints for each one.	*Other Types of Evaluation Situations and Blueprints* Explain the variety of evaluation situations and why you have chosen them. Explain how you designed the "Test Blueprints" for each situation, including the learning objectives and material covered, how you allocated points, and the level of cognition required.
Assignments and Rubrics Describe in detail all assignments with accompanying rubrics specifying quality indicators. You may provide in the syllabus short descriptions of assignments and provide full explanations and rubrics in a separate document.	*Assignments and Rubrics* Explain why you chose these assignments, why you selected the quality indicators for the rubrics you developed, and the opportunities your students will have to practice and receive feedback without assessment. If you plan to grade in-class efforts ("participation"), provide a rubric describing exactly what you expect students to do. Be sure to list those efforts in your teaching goals and learning objectives and to plan activities to help your students learn and receive feedback on those activities.
Classroom Assessment Techniques Create and describe Classroom Assessment Techniques that provide you with feedback on classroom content, process, and ambiance.	*Classroom Assessment Techniques* Explain why you created these Classroom Assessment Techniques to provide you with feedback on classroom content, process, and ambiance.
Student and Peer Feedback Include student and peer feedback you have received about your teaching in this particular course. Summarize each instance of feedback with strengths and weaknesses.	*Student and Peer Feedback* Describe your reaction and whether or not you agree with the feedback you received. Describe your efforts or intentions to address any weaknesses and to continue the strengths.
Student Work Include samples of student work from previous times you have taught this course. Samples should include excellent, good, and poor examples with your comments/feedback to your students.	*Student Work* Describe the samples in terms of your teaching goals and course learning objectives.

Revised Teaching Goals Inventory

I have found that the best method for selecting teaching goals (TGs) is the Teaching Goals Inventory (TGI), designed by Angelo and Cross (1993), in their book *Classroom Assessment Techniques*. The TGI has six clusters: higher-order thinking skills, basic academic success, discipline-specific knowledge and skills, liberal arts and academic values, work and career preparation, and personal development. The listing of TGs in the TGI is by those clusters, rather than in a developmental structure. Having included the TGI in dozens of courses and with hundreds of workshop participants, I have modified and added to it in order to make it more useful for helping course designers choose goals for the developmental level of their students. The adaptation places TGs in the order in which they would be appropriate in the Bloom taxonomies. Some of the Angelo and Cross TGs appear in more than one taxonomy, and several of the levels do not have a TG in the Angelo and Cross inventory.

Sample Teaching Goals by Bloom Levels

SAMPLE TEACHING GOALS BY BLOOM LEVELS
Cognitive Taxonomy (Anderson & Krathwohl, 2001)

Cognitive Process Dimension						
Knowledge Dimension	1. Remember	2. Understand	3. Apply	4. Analyze	5. Evaluate	6. Create
A. Factual Knowledge	Learn terms/facts of this subject (18).	Describe terms/facts of this subject.	Apply facts already learned to new problems/ situations.	Develop ability to integrate information and ideas (5).	Develop ability to distinguish between fact and opinion (8).	Discover new facts.
B. Conceptual Knowledge	Learn concepts/ theories of this subject (19).	Develop ability to draw reasonable inferences from observations (4).	Apply principles/ theories already learned to new problems/ situations (1).	Develop analytic skills (2).	Develop an informed historical perspective (32).	Develop ability to think creatively (7).
C. Procedural Knowledge	Develop skill in using materials, tools, and/or technology central to this subject (20).	Learn techniques/ methods used to gain new knowledge in this subject (23).	Develop problem-solving skills (3).	Develop capacity to make informed choices (35).	Learn to evaluate methods/materials of this subject (24).	Create new procedures.
D. Meta-Cognitive Knowledge	Learn aspects of own learning style.	Learn techniques/ methods to improve own learning in this subject.	Improve learning skills (11–16).	Analyze application of learning styles to specific knowledge.	Evaluate learning methods in specific areas of knowledge.	Create new ways to learn.

Note. Laurie Richlin (2005), laurie.richlin@cgu.edu. Adapted from *Revised Bloom Taxonomy* by J. McFann, 2005, presentation at the Southern California Professional Developers' Learning Community, Claremont, CA; and *A Taxonomy for Learning, Teaching, and Assessing: A Revision of Bloom's Taxonomy of Educational Objectives,* by L. W. Anderson and D. R. Krathwohl (Eds.), 2001, New York: Addison Wesley Longman. Used by permission. Numbers in parentheses are TG numbers in Angelo and Cross (1993). Some Angelo and Cross TGs appear in more than one taxonomy. TGs without numbers are by Richlin.

Affective Taxonomy (Krathwhol, Bloom, & Masia, 1964)

RECEIVING PHENOMENA: Willingness to hear.

1.1	Develop an openness to new ideas (27)

RESPONDING TO PHENOMENA: Motivation to attend and react.

2.1	Follow directions/instructions/plans (40)

VALUING: Worth placed on object, phenomenon, or behavior.

3.1	Develop an appreciation of the liberal arts and sciences (26)
3.2	Develop an informed appreciation of other cultures (34)
3.3	Develop aesthetic appreciation (31)
3.4	Develop a lifelong love of learning (30)

ORGANIZING VALUES: Prioritizes (compares) values.

4.1	Cultivate an active commitment to honesty (50)
4.2	Learn to understand perspectives and values of this subject (21)
4.3	Develop capacity to think for self (51)

INTERNALIZING VALUES: Values control behavior.

5.1	Develop a commitment to exercise the rights and responsibilities of citizenship (29)
5.2	Develop an informed concern about contemporary social issues (28)
5.3	Develop a commitment to personal achievement (42)
5.4	Develop capacity to make informed ethical choices (35)
5.5	Develop capacity to make wise decisions (52)
5.6	Cultivate a sense of responsibility for one's own behavior (44)
5.7	Work productively with others (36)

Psychomotor Taxonomy (Dave, 1970)

IMITATION: Copies actions.

1.1	Repeat actions
1.2	Copy examples
1.3	Improve skills: paying attention (9), concentration (10), memory (11), listening (12), speaking (13), reading (14), writing (15), study (16), mathematical (17)

MANIPULATION: Reproduces activity from memory

2.1	Build object after demonstration

PRECISION: Execute skill independent of help

3.1	Demonstrate ability to perform independently

ARTICULATION: Adapt and integrate

4.1	Combine moves to meet new requirements

NATURALIZATION: Automated mastery of skills at strategic level

5.1	Develop ability to perform skillfully (43)

Grasha-Reichmann Student Learning Style Scales

Self-scoring version available online at
http://www.iats.com/publications/GLSI.html

The following questionnaire has been designed to help you clarify your attitudes and feelings toward learning in college. There are no right or wrong answers to each question. However, as you answer each question, form your answers with regard to your general attitudes and feelings toward all of your courses.

Respond to the items listed below by using the following scale. Put your answers on the answer sheet that is provided.

Use a rating of 1 if you *strongly disagree* with the statement.
Use a rating of 2 if you *moderately disagree* with the statement.
Use a rating of 3 if you are *undecided.*
Use a rating of 4 if you *moderately agree* with the statement.
Use a rating of 5 if you *strongly agree* with the statement.

1. I prefer to work by myself on assignments in my courses.
2. I often daydream during class.
3. Working with other students on class activities is something I enjoy doing.
4. I like it whenever teachers clearly state what is required and expected.
5. To do well, it is necessary to compete with other students for the teacher's attention.
6. I do whatever is asked of me to learn the content in my classes.
7. My ideas about the content are often as good as those in the textbook.
8. Classroom activities are usually boring.
9. I enjoy discussing my ideas about the course content with other students.
10. I rely on my teachers to tell me what is important for me to learn.
11. It is necessary to compete with other students to get a good grade.
12. Class sessions typically are worth attending.
13. I study what is important to me and not always what the instructor says is important.
14. I very seldom am excited about material covered in a course.
15. I enjoy hearing what other students think about issues raised in class.
16. I only do what I am absolutely required to do in my courses.

17. In class, I must compete with other students to get my ideas across.
18. I get more out of going to class than staying at home.
19. I learn a lot of the content in my classes on my own.
20. I don't want to attend most of my classes.
21. Students should be encouraged to share more of their ideas with each other.
22. I complete assignments exactly the way my teachers tell me to do them.
23. Students have to be aggressive to do well in courses.
24. It is my responsibility to get as much as I can out of a course.
25. I feel very confident in my ability to learn on my own.
26. Paying attention during class sessions is very difficult for me to do.
27. I like to study for tests with other students.
28. I do not like making choices about what to study or how to do assignments.
29. I like to solve problems or answer questions before anyone else can.
30. Classroom activities are interesting.
31. I like to develop my own ideas about course content.
32. I have given up trying to learn anything by going to class.
33. Class sessions make me feel like a part of a team where people help each other learn.
34. Students should be more closely supervised by teachers on course projects.
35. To get ahead in class, it is necessary to step on the toes of other students.
36. I try to participate as much as I can in all aspects of a course.
37. I have my own ideas about how classes should be run.
38. I study just hard enough to get by.
39. An important part of taking courses is learning to get along with other people.
40. My notes contain almost everything the teacher said in class.
41. Being one of the best students in my classes is very important to me.
42. I do all course assignments well whether or not I think they are interesting.
43. If I like a topic, I try to find out more about it on my own.
44. I typically cram for exams.
45. Learning the material is a cooperative effort between students and teachers.
46. I prefer class sessions that are highly organized.
47. To stand out in my classes, I complete the assignments better than other students.
48. I typically complete course assignments before their deadlines.
49. I like classes where I can work at my own pace.
50. I would prefer that teachers ignore me in class.
51. I am willing to help out other students when they do not understand something.
52. Students should be told exactly what material is to be covered on the exams.
53. I like to know how well other students are doing on exams and course assignments.
54. I complete required assignments as well as those that are optional.
55. When I don't understand something, I try to figure it out for myself.
56. During class sessions, I tend to socialize with people sitting next to me.
57. I enjoy participating in small group activities during class.
58. I like it when teachers are well organized for a session.
59. I want my teachers to give me more recognition for the good work I do.
60. In my classes, I often sit toward the front of the room.

LEARNING STYLE SCORING KEY

1) Copy your responses from the sheet of paper with your ratings on it to the space provided below for each item.

Learning Style Test Items

1._____.	2._____.	3._____.	4._____.	5._____.	6._____.
7._____.	8._____.	9._____.	10._____.	11._____.	12._____.
13._____.	14._____.	15._____.	16._____.	17._____.	18._____.
19._____.	20._____.	21._____.	22._____.	23._____.	24._____.
25._____.	26._____.	27._____.	28._____.	29._____.	30._____.
31._____.	32._____.	33._____.	34._____.	35._____.	36._____.
37._____.	38._____.	39._____.	40._____.	41._____.	42._____.
43._____.	44._____.	45._____.	46._____.	47._____.	48._____.
49._____.	50._____.	51._____.	52._____.	53._____.	54._____.
55._____.	56._____.	57._____.	58._____.	59._____.	60._____.

2) Sum your ratings for each column and place them in the spaces below

._____.   ._____.   ._____.   ._____.   ._____.   ._____.

3) Divide your total score for each column by 10 and place your answer in the spaces below

._____.   ._____.   ._____.   ._____.   ._____.   ._____.

Independent   Avoidant   Collaborative   Dependent   Competitive   Participant

4) The names for each learning style associated with each column are shown above.

5) Check whether your score represents a relatively Low, Moderate, or High score based on the norms for each learning style scale shown below.

	Low	Moderate	High
Independent	[1.0–2.7]	[2.8–3.8]	[3.9–5.0]
Avoidant	[1.0–1.8]	[1.9–3.1]	[3.2–5.0]
Collaborative	[1.0–2.7]	[2.8–3.4]	[3.5–5.0]
Dependent	[1.0–2.9]	[3.0–4.0]	[4.1–5.0]
Competitive	[1.0–1.7]	[1.8–2.8]	[2.9–5.0]
Participant	[1.0–3.0]	[3.1–4.1]	[4.2–5.0]

Note. From *Teaching with Style: A Practical Guide to Enhancing Learning by Understanding Teaching and Learning Styles* (pp. 201–203), by A. F. Grasha, 1996, Claremont, CA: Alliance (www.iats.com). Reproduced by permission.

Grasha Teaching Styles Inventory: Version 3.0

Self-scoring version available online at
http://www.iats.com/publications/TSI.html

To complete the Teaching Styles Inventory you will need to choose an undergraduate or graduate course you currently teach, have taught, or are planning to teach.

Brief Title of Course: _____

Primary Level of This Course

Freshmen _____ Sophomore _____ Junior _____ Senior _____

Beginning graduate level course _____ Advanced graduate level course _____

Is this course required for undergraduate majors and/or a graduate degree?

Yes _____ No _____

What is the average enrollment in the course? _____

How many times have you taught this class? _____

Respond to each of the items below in terms of how they apply to the course you have chosen. Answer as honestly and as objectively as you can. Resist the temptation to respond as you believe you "should or ought to think or behave" or in terms of what you believe is the "expected or proper thing to do." Put your answers on the answer sheet that is provided. *Respond to the items on the following pages by using the following scale.*

1	2	3	4	5	6	7
Strongly Disagree	Somewhat Disagree		Neither Disagree or Agree	Somewhat Agree		Strongly Agree

Very Unimportant Aspect of My   Very Important Aspect of My
Approach to Teaching This Course   Approach to Teaching This Course

1. Facts, concepts, and principles are the most important things that students should acquire.

2. I set high standards for students in this class.

3. What I say and do models appropriate ways for students to think about issues in the content.

4. My teaching goals and methods address a variety of student learning styles.

5. Students typically work on course projects alone with little supervision from me.

6. Sharing my knowledge and expertise with students is very important to me.

7. I give students negative feedback when their performance is unsatisfactory.

8. Students are encouraged to emulate the example I provide.

9. I spend time consulting with students on how to improve their work on individual and/or group projects.

10. Activities in this class encourage students to develop their own ideas about content issues.

11. What I have to say about a topic is important for students to acquire a broader perspective on the issues in that area.

12. Students would describe my standard and expectation as somewhat strict and rigid.

13. I typically show students how and what to do in order to master course content.

14. Small group discussions are employed to help students develop their ability to think critically.

15. Students design one or more self-directed learning experiences.

16. I want students to leave this course well prepared for further work in this area.

17. It is my responsibility to define what students must learn and how they should learn it.

18. Examples from my personal experiences often are used to illustrate points about the material.

19. I guide students' work on course projects by asking questions, exploring options, and suggesting alternative ways to do things.

20. Developing the ability of students to think and work independently is an important goal.

21. Lecturing is a significant part of how I teach each of the class sessions.

22. I provide very clear guidelines for how I want tasks completed in this course.

23. I often show students how they can use various concepts and principles.

24. Course activities encourage students to take the initiative and responsibility for their learning.

25. Students take responsibility for teaching part of the class sessions.

26. My expertise is typically used to resolve disagreements about contentious issues.

27. This course has very specific goals and objectives that I want to accomplish.

28. Students receive frequent verbal and/or written comments on their performance.

29. I solicit student advice about how and what to teach in this course.

30. Students set their own pace for completing independent and/or group projects.

31. Students might describe me as a "storehouse of knowledge" who dispenses the facts, principles, and concepts they need.

32. My expectations for what I want students to do are clearly stated in the syllabus.

33. Eventually, many students begin to think like me about the course content.

34. Students can make choices among activities in order to complete course requirements.

35. My approach to teaching is similar to a manager of a work group who delegates tasks and responsibilities to subordinates.

36. I have more material in this course than I have time to cover.

37. My standards and expectations help students develop the discipline they need to learn.

38. Students might describe me as a "coach" who works closely with someone to correct problems in how they think and behave.

39. I give students a lot of personal support and encouragement to do well in this course.

40. I assume the role of a resource problem who is available to students whenever they need help.

TEACHING STYLE SCORING KEY

1) Copy the rating you assigned to each item in the spaces provided below.

1. _____ .	2. _____ .	3. _____ .	4. _____ .	5. _____ .
6. _____ .	7. _____ .	8. _____ .	9. _____ .	10. _____ .
11. _____ .	12. _____ .	13. _____ .	14. _____ .	15. _____ .
16. _____ .	17. _____ .	18. _____ .	19. _____ .	20. _____ .
21. _____ .	22. _____ .	23. _____ .	24. _____ .	25. _____ .
26. _____ .	27. _____ .	28. _____ .	29. _____ .	30. _____ .
31. _____ .	32. _____ .	33. _____ .	34. _____ .	35. _____ .
36. _____ .	37. _____ .	38. _____ .	39. _____ .	40. _____ .

2) Sum the rating for each column and place the total in the spaces below

. _____ .   . _____ .   . _____ .   . _____ .   . _____ .

3) Divide each column score above by 8 to obtain the average numerical rating you assigned to the items associated with each teaching style. Place your average rating to the nearest decimal point in the spaces below

. _____ .   . _____ .   . _____ .   . _____ .   . _____ .

Expert	Formal Authority	Personal Model	Facilitator	Delegator

4) The teaching style that corresponds to each column is shown above.

5) Range of low, moderate, and high scores for each style based on the test norms.

	Low	Moderate	High
Expert	[1.0–3.2]	[3.3–4.8]	[4.9–7.0]
Formal Authority	[1.0–4.0]	[4.1–5.4]	[5.5–7.0]
Personal Model	[1.0–4.3]	[4.4–5.7]	[5.8–7.0]
Facilitator	[1.0–3.7]	[3.8–5.3]	[5.4–7.0]
Delegator	[1.0–2.6]	[2.7–4.2]	[4.3–7.0]

From *Teaching with Style: A Practical Guide to Enhancing Learning by Understanding Teaching and Learning Styles* (pp. 160–164), by A. F. Grasha, 1996, Claremont, CA: Alliance (www.iats.com). Used by permission.

Instructional Script

Instructor: _____

Course: _____

Section Learning Objectives.

Students completing this session will be able to:

1.

2.

3.

Time Line	Content	Stage Directions	Learning Experiences	Diversity Check	Materials	A/V

Society for Teaching and Learning in Higher Education Ethical Principles in University Teaching

STLHE Authors

Harry Murray (1992 3M Fellow), Eileen Gillese (1986 3M Fellow), Madeline Lennon (1990 3M Fellow), Paul Mercer (1994 3M Fellow), Marilyn Robinson (1993 3M Fellow)

With the endorsement of the following 3M Fellows:

Arshad Ahmad * Frank Aherne * Guy Allen * Wiktor Askanas * Colin Baird * Roger Beck * David Bentley * Beverly Cameron * Norman Cameron * Thomas Cleary * William Coleman * James Erskine * Graham Fishburne * Joyce Forbes * Dean Gaily * Allan Gedalof * William Gilsdorf * Joseph Habowsky * Ralph Johnson * Peter Kennedy * Ralph Krueger * Estelle Lacoursiere * Gordon Lange * Jack London * Nadia Mikhael * Alex Middleton * James Newton * Gary Poole * Manfred Prokop * Pat Rogers * Peter Rosati * Robert Schulz * Ronald Sheese * Alan Slavin * Ronald Smith * Lois Stanford * Susan Stanton * David Topper * Donald Ursino * Fred Vermeulen * Wayne Weston

Preamble

The purpose of this document is to provide a set of basic ethical principles that define the professional responsibilities of university professors in their role as teachers.

Ethical principles are conceptualized here as general guidelines, ideals, or expectations that need to be taken into account, along with other relevant conditions and circumstances, in the design and analysis of university teaching.

The intent of this document is not to provide a list of ironclad rules, or a systematic code of conduct, along with prescribed penalties for infractions, that will automatically apply in all situations and govern all eventualities. Similarly, the intent is not to contradict the concept of academic freedom, but rather to describe ways in which academic freedom can be exercised in a responsible manner.

Finally, the present document is intended only as a first approximation, or as 'food for thought', not necessarily as a final product that is ready for adoption in the absence of discussion and consideration of local needs.

Ethical Principles in University Teaching was developed by the Society for Teaching and Learning in Higher Education, and is endorsed by the winners of the national 3M teaching award whose names appear on the cover page. The document was created by individuals actively involved in university teaching, and will be distributed to university professors across Canada with the support of 3M Canada.

The Society for Teaching and Learning in Higher Education (STLHE) believes that implementation of an ethical code similar to that described herein will be advantageous to university teachers (e.g., in removing ambiguity concerning teaching responsibilities); and will contribute significantly to improvement of teaching. For these reasons, STLHE recommends that the document be discussed thoroughly at Canadian universities, with input from professors, students, and administrators, and that universities consider adopting or implementing ethical principles of teaching similar to those described in this document.

Principle 1: Content Competence

A university teacher maintains a high level of subject matter knowledge and ensures that course content is current, accurate, representative, and appropriate to the position of the course within the student's program of studies.

This principle means that a teacher is responsible for maintaining (or acquiring) subject matter competence not only in areas of personal interest but in all areas relevant to course goals or objectives. Appropriateness of course content implies that what is actually taught in the course is consistent with stated course objectives and prepares students adequately for subsequent courses for which the present course is a prerequisite. Representativeness of course content implies that for topics involving difference of opinion or interpretation, representative points of view are acknowledged and placed in perspective. Achievement of content competence requires that the teacher take active steps to be up-to-date in content areas relevant to his or her courses; to be informed of the content of prerequisite courses and of courses for which the teacher's course is prerequisite; and to provide adequate representation of important topic areas and points of view.

Specific examples of failure to fulfill the principle of content competence occur when an instructor teaches subjects for which she or he has an insufficient knowledge base, when an instructor misinterprets research evidence to support a theory or social policy favored by the instructor, or when an instructor responsible for a prerequisite survey course teaches only those topics in which the instructor has a personal interest.

Principle 2: Pedagogical Competence

A pedagogically competent teacher communicates the objectives of the course to students, is aware of al-

ternative instructional methods or strategies, and selects methods of instruction that, according to research evidence (including personal or self-reflective research), are effective in helping students to achieve the course objectives.

This principle implies that, in addition to knowing the subject matter, a teacher has adequate pedagogical knowledge and skills, including communication of objectives, selection of effective instructional methods, providing opportunity for practice and feedback, and dealing with student diversity. If mastery of a certain skill (e.g., critical analysis, design of experiments) is part of the course objectives and will be considered in evaluation and grading of students, the teacher provides students with adequate opportunity to practice and receive feedback on that skill during the course. If learning styles differ significantly for different students or groups of students, the teacher is aware of these differences and, if feasible, varies her or his style of teaching accordingly.

To maintain pedagogical competence, an instructor takes active steps to stay current regarding teaching strategies that will help students learn relevant knowledge and skills and will provide equal educational opportunity for diverse groups. This might involve reading general or discipline-specific educational literature, attending workshops and conferences, or experimentation with alternative methods of teaching a given course or a specific group of students.

Specific examples of failure to fulfill the principle of pedagogical competence include using an instructional method or assessment method that is incongruent with the stated course objectives (e.g., using exams consisting solely of fact-memorization questions when the main objective of the course is to teach problem-solving skills); and failing to give students adequate opportunity to practice or learn skills that are included in the course objectives and will be tested on the final exam.

Principle 3: Dealing With Sensitive Topics

Topics that students are likely to find sensitive or discomforting are dealt with in an open, honest, and positive way.

Among other things, this principle means that the teacher acknowledges from the outset that a particular topic is sensitive, and explains why it is necessary to include it in the course syllabus. Also, the teacher identifies his or her own perspective on the issue and compares it to alternative approaches or interpretations, thereby providing students with an understanding of the complexity of the issue and the difficulty of achieving a single "objective" conclusion. Finally, in order to provide a safe and open environment for class discussion, the teacher invites all students to state their position on the issue, sets ground rules for discussion, is respectful of students even when it is necessary to disagree, and encourages students to be respectful of one another.

As one example of a sensitive topic, analysis of certain poems written by John Donne can cause distress among students who perceive racial slurs embedded in the professor's interpretation, particularly if the latter is presented as the authoritative reading of the poem. As a result, some students may view the class as closed and exclusive rather than open and inclusive. A reasonable option is for the professor's analysis of the poem to be followed by an open class discussion of other possible interpretations and the pros and cons of each.

Another example of a sensitive topic occurs when a film depicting scenes of child abuse is shown, without forewarning, in a developmental psychology class. Assuming that such a film has a valid pedagogical role, student distress and discomfort can be minimized by warning students in advance of the content of the film, explaining why it is included in the curriculum, and providing opportunities for students to discuss their reactions to the film.

Principle 4: Student Development

The overriding responsibility of the teacher is to contribute to the intellectual development of the student, at least in the context of the teacher's own area of expertise, and to avoid actions such as exploitation and discrimination that detract from student development.

According to this principle, the teacher's most basic responsibility is to design instruction that facilitates learning and encourages autonomy and independent thinking in students, to treat students with respect and dignity, and to avoid actions that detract unjustifiably from student development. Failure to take responsibility for student development occurs when a teacher comes to class under-prepared, fails to design effective instruction, coerces students to adopt a particular value or point of view, or fails to discuss alternative theoretical interpretations (see also Principles 1, 2, and 3).

Less obvious examples of failure to take responsibility for student development can arise when teachers ignore the power differential between themselves and students and behave in ways that exploit or denigrate

students. Such behaviors include sexual or racial discrimination; derogatory comments toward students; taking primary or sole authorship of a publication reporting research conceptualized, designed, and conducted by a student collaborator; failure to acknowledge academic or intellectual debts to students; and assigning research work to students that serves the ends of the teacher but is unrelated to the educational goals of the course.

In some cases, the teacher's responsibility to contribute to student development can come into conflict with responsibilities to other agencies, such as the university, the academic discipline, or society as a whole. This can happen, for example, when a marginal student requests a letter of reference in support of advanced education, or when a student with learning disabilities requests accommodations that require modification of normal grading standards or graduation requirements. There are no hard and fast rules that govern situations such as these. The teacher must weigh all conflicting responsibilities, possibly consult with other individuals, and come to a reasoned decision.

Principle 5: Dual Relationships With Students

To avoid conflict of interest, a teacher does not enter into dual-role relationships with students that are likely to detract from student development or lead to actual or perceived favouritism on the part of the teacher.

This principle means that it is the responsibility of the teacher to keep relationships with students focused on pedagogical goals and academic requirements. The most obvious example of a dual relationship that is likely to impair teacher objectivity and/or detract from student development is any form of sexual or close personal relationship with a current student. Other potentially problematic dual relationships include: accepting a teaching (or grading) role with respect to a member of one's immediate family, a close friend, or an individual who is also a client, patient, or business partner; excessive socializing with students outside of class, either individually or as a group; lending money to or borrowing money from students; giving gifts to or accepting gifts from students; and introducing a course requirement that students participate in a political movement advocated by the instructor. Even if the teacher believes that she or he is maintaining objectivity in situations such as these, the perception of favoritism on the part of other students is as educationally disastrous as actual favoritism or unfairness. If a teacher does become involved in a dual relationship with a student, despite efforts to the contrary, it is the responsibility of the teacher to notify his or her supervisor of the situation as soon as possible, so that alternative arrangements can be made for supervision or evaluation of the student.

Although there are definite pedagogical benefits to establishing good rapport with students and interacting with students both inside and outside the classroom, there are also serious risks of exploitation, compromise of academic standards, and harm to student development. It is the responsibility of the teacher to prevent these risks from materializing into real or perceived conflicts of interest.

Principle 6: **Confidentiality**

Student grades, attendance records, and private communications are treated as confidential materials, and are released only with student consent, or for legitimate academic purposes, or if there are reasonable grounds for believing that releasing such information will be beneficial to the student or will prevent harm to others.

This principle suggests that students are entitled to the same level of confidentiality in their relationships with teachers as would exist in a lawyer-client or doctor-patient relationship. Violation of confidentiality in the teacher-student relationship can cause students to distrust teachers and to show decreased academic motivation. Whatever rules or policies are followed with respect to confidentiality of student records, these should be disclosed in full to students at the beginning of the academic term.

It could be argued that in the absence of adequate grounds (i.e., student consent, legitimate purpose, or benefit to student) any of the following could be construed as a violation of confidentiality: providing student academic records to a potential employer, researcher, or private investigator; discussing a student's grades or academic problems with another faculty member; and using privately communicated student experiences as teaching or research materials. Similarly, leaving graded student papers or exams in a pile outside one's office makes it possible for any student to determine any other student's grade and thus fails to protect the confidentiality of individual student grades. This problem can be avoided by having students pick up their papers individually during office hours, or by returning papers with no grade or identifying information visible on the cover page.

Principle 7: **Respect for Colleagues**

A university teacher respects the dignity of her or his colleagues and works cooperatively with colleagues in the interest of fostering student development.

This principle means that in interactions among colleagues with respect to teaching, the overriding concern is the development of students. Disagreements between colleagues relating to teaching are settled privately, if possible, with no harm to student development. If a teacher suspects that a colleague has shown incompetence or ethical violations in teaching, the teacher takes responsibility for investigating the matter thoroughly and consulting privately with the colleague before taking further action.

A specific example of failure to show respect for colleagues occurs when a teacher makes unwarranted derogatory comments in the classroom about the competence of another teacher . . . for example, Professor A tells students that information provided to them last year by Professor B is of no use and will be replaced by information from Professor A in the course at hand. Other examples of failure to uphold this principle would be for a curriculum committee to refuse to require courses in other departments that compete with their own department for student enrolment; or for Professor X to refuse a student permission to take a course from Professor Y, who is disliked by Professor X, even though the course would be useful to the student.

Principle 8: **Valid Assessment of Students**

Given the importance of assessment of student performance in university teaching and in students' lives and careers, instructors are responsible for taking adequate steps to ensure that assessment of students is valid, open, fair, and congruent with course objectives.

This principle means that the teacher is aware of research (including personal or self-reflective research) on the advantages and disadvantages of alternative methods of assessment, and based on this knowledge, the teacher selects assessment techniques that are consistent with the objectives of the course and at the same time are as reliable and valid as possible. Furthermore, assessment procedures and grading standards are communicated clearly to students at the beginning of the course, and except in rare circumstances, there is no deviation from the announced procedures. Student exams, papers, and assignments are graded carefully and fairly through the use of a rational marking system that can be communicated to students. By means appropriate for the size of the class, students are provided with prompt and accurate feedback on their performance at regular intervals throughout the course, an explanation as to how their work was graded, and constructive suggestions as to how to improve their standing in the course. In a similar vein, teachers are fair and objective in writing letters of reference for students.

One example of an ethically questionable assessment practice is to grade students on skills that were not part of the announced course objectives and/or were not allocated adequate practice opportunity during the course. If students are expected to demonstrate critical inquiry skills on the final exam, they should have been given the opportunity to develop critical inquiry skills during the course. Another violation of valid assessment occurs when faculty members teaching two different sections of the same course use drastically different assessment procedures or grading standards, such that the same level of student performance earns significantly different final grades in the two sections.

Principle 9: **Respect for Institution**

In the interests of student development, a university teacher is aware of and respects the educational goals, policies, and standards of the institution in which he or she teaches.

This principle implies that a teacher shares a collective responsibility to work for the good of the university as a whole, to uphold the educational goals and standards of the university, and to abide by university policies and regulations pertaining to the education of students.

Specific examples of failure to uphold the principle of respect for institution include engaging in excessive work activity outside the university that conflicts with university teaching responsibilities; and being unaware of or ignoring valid university regulations on provision of course outlines, scheduling of exams, or academic misconduct.

References

The authors are indebted to the following for ideas that were incorporated into the present document:

American Psychological Association (1990). Ethical principles of psychologists. *American Psychologist*, 45, 390–395.

University of Calgary (1994). *Code of Professional Ethics for Academic Staff*.

Matthews, J. R. (1991). The teaching of ethics and the ethics of teaching. *Teaching of Psychology*, 18, 80–85.

Published by:

Society for Teaching and Learning in Higher Education
University of British Columbia
Centre for Teaching and Academic Growth
6326 Agricultural Road
Vancouver, B.C., CANADA V6T 1Z2
Telephone: (604) 822-9149
Fax: (604) 822-9826
Email: Gary.Poole@ubc.ca

Rubrics for Portfolio

This resource provides the following rubrics:

- Course Description

- Teaching Goals and Learning Objectives

- Explanation of Design Choices

- In-Class Learning Experiences (Script)

- Assignment

- Rubric

- Grading Plan

- Blueprint for Tests/Other Evaluation

- Classroom Assessment Techniques (CATs)

- Teaching><Learning Philosophy for Course

RUBRIC FOR COURSE DESCRIPTION
Developed with Al Arboleda, LaMesha Carter, and Akiko Otsu

CATEGORY	7–10	4–6	1–3	0
Marketing	Describes course in exciting way that motivates student participation	Describes course in interesting terms that will motivate some students	Description has few motivational qualities	Description is dry and not motivating
Hopes and Dreams	Clearly describes instructor's hopes and dreams for students' relationship to course material	Describes hopes and dreams for students' relationship to this course, but need additional explanation	Vaguely describes hopes and dreams	No description of hopes and dreams
Course Content	Course content, topics are well described	Course content, topics generally described	Course content, topics are vague	Course content, topics are not mentioned
"Big Questions" Connection to Course	Clearly describes relationship of discipline's "big questions" to course	Describes relationship of discipline's "big questions" to course	Vaguely describes relationship of discipline's "big questions" to course	No description of relationship of discipline's "big questions" to course
Connects Course to Development of Student Abilities	Clearly describes what students will be able to do after completing course	Describes what students will be able to do after completing course	Vaguely describes what students will be able to do after completing course	No description of what students will be able to do after completing course
Course Level	Clearly explains levels, majors, and interests for which this course is designed	Explains some levels, majors, and interests for which this course is designed	Partially explains levels, majors, and interests for which this course is designed	Not discussed
Prerequisites	Includes all prerequisites, clearly stating why they are required	Does not include all prerequisites or has little explanation	Includes few prerequisites and/or no explanation	Not discussed
Course Type, Term, and Frequency	Fully describes type of course, when course is offered, and meeting frequency	Partially describes type of course, when course is offered, and meeting frequency	Describes little about type of course, when course is offered, or meeting frequency	Not discussed

RUBRIC FOR TEACHING GOALS AND LEARNING OBJECTIVES
Created by John Alexander and Nathan Garrett
Teaching Goals Rubric—Repeat for Each Goal

Points	Criteria
1	TG stems from the course hopes and dreams.
1	TG is at a reasonable cognitive level for the students in the course.
1	TG has one or more learning objectives.

Rubric for Individual Learning Objectives—Repeat for Each Objective

Points	Criteria
1	LO stems from a course or teaching goal.
2	LO contains a directly observable and measurable action verb (such as list, identity, solve, propose, assess).
1	LO is about a single, discrete, and focused outcome.
1	LO is clear and understandable.

Compute Teaching Goals and Learning Objectives Points	
Total Potential Points **5 multiplied by the number of LOs + 3 multiplied by the number of TGs**	
Total Earned Points Sum all LO- and TG-awarded points.	
Overall Percentage Divide awarded points by potential points.	
Points Multiply percentage by 75.	

RUBRIC FOR EXPLANATION OF DESIGN CHOICES

CATEGORY	4	3	2	1	0
Design Elements 30%	All design elements are addressed and all explanations have at least 5 sentences about each.	Most elements are addressed and are explained with at least 5 sentences about each.	Some elements are described but are described with fewer than 5 sentences about each.	Few elements are explained.	No elements are explained.
Student Focus 30%	Explanation clearly relates to student learning and includes several supporting details and/or examples.	Explanation relates to student learning but provides few supporting details and/or examples.	Explanation relates to student learning but provides no details or examples.	Explanation has little to do with student learning.	Explanation has nothing to do with student learning.
Knowledge Base 20%	All design elements are supported by learning theory.	Most elements are supported by learning theory.	Some elements are supported by learning theory.	Few elements are supported by learning theory.	Elements are not supported by learning theory.
Sources 10%	All sources are accurately documented in the desired format.	Many sources are accurately documented, but a few are not in the desired format.	Some sources are accurately documented, but many are not in the desired format.	Few sources are accurately documented.	Sources are not accurately documented.
Mechanics 10%	There are no grammatical, spelling, or punctuation errors.	There are a few grammatical, spelling, or punctuation errors.	There are some grammatical, spelling, or punctuation errors, but explanation can be understood.	There are many grammatical, spelling, or punctuation errors, but explanation can be understood.	There are many grammatical, spelling, or punctuation errors, and explanation cannot be understood.

RUBRIC FOR IN-CLASS LEARNING EXPERIENCES (SCRIPT)

CATEGORY	8–10	4–7	1–4	0
Times	All times are appropriate to the importance of the material.	Some times are appropriate to the importance of the material.	Times are not appropriate to the importance of the material.	Times are not listed.
Content Clarity	Content is clearly described.	Some content is clearly described.	Content is not clearly described.	Content is not included.
Content Appropriateness	All content relates to learning objectives.	Some of the content relates to learning objectives.	Little of the content relates to learning objectives.	No content relates to learning objectives.
Activity	All activities support learning objectives/content.	Most activities support learning objectives/content.	Some activities support learning objectives/content.	Activities do not support learning objectives/content.
Diversity Check Teaching Style and Learning Style	Activities appropriately mix styles for maximum student learning.	Activities have some mix of styles for student learning.	Activities do not mix styles for maximum student learning.	Diversity check is not listed.

RUBRIC FOR ASSIGNMENT

Created by Marlene Biseda and Ariana Brooks

CATEGORY	4	3	2	1	0
Assignment Link to Learning Objectives (LOs)	Assignment is clearly linked to LOs.	Assignment is linked to LOs but not clearly stated.	There appears to be a link between the assignment and LOs.	There is an unclear link between assignment and LOs.	Assignment is not linked to LOs.
Assignment Purpose	Purpose of the assignment is clearly defined.	Most aspects of the purpose are clearly defined.	Some aspects of the purpose are clearly defined.	Few aspects of the purpose are clearly defined.	Purpose of the assignment is not clearly defined.
Assignment Objectives	Overall task and subtask objectives (if appropriate) are clearly explained.	Task is broken down by objectives appropriately and most objectives (>50%) are clearly defined.	Task is broken down appropriately and some objectives (about 50%) are clearly defined.	Task is not broken down appropriately or few objectives (<50%) are clearly defined.	Task is not broken down into the appropriate objectives and these objectives are not clearly defined.
Assignment Parameters, Penalties, and Due Dates	Assignment parameters, penalties, and due dates are clearly defined.	Only two of the elements are clearly defined OR all three are defined but unclear.	Only one of the elements is clearly defined OR two are defined but unclear.	Only one of the elements is defined but unclear.	Assignment parameters, penalties, and due dates are not defined.
Assignment Values	Value of the assignment and value of its tasks are clearly indicated.	Value of the assignment OR its tasks are clearly indicated.	Value of the assignment OR its tasks are indicated but unclear.	Value of the assignment OR its tasks are not indicated.	Value of the assignment and its tasks are not indicated.
Assignment Level	Assignment is appropriate to student level.	Assignment is close to student level.	Assignment is appropriate for some students.	Assignment is appropriate for a few students.	Assignment is not appropriate to student level.

RUBRIC FOR RUBRIC
Created by Marlene Biseda and Ariana Brooks

CATEGORY	4	3	2	1	0
Rubric Categories Uniqueness	Rubric has unique assessment categories.	Most of the assessment categories (>50%) are unique but a few overlap with others.	Some of the assessment categories (about 50%) are unique but some overlap with others.	Few of the assessment categories (<50%) are unique; most overlap with others.	Rubric categories are not unique and overlap each other.
Rubric Category Objectives	Assessment categories account for all task and subtask objectives factors of the learning experience.	Assessment categories account for most of the relative factors of the learning experience.	Assessment categories account for some of the relative factors of the learning experience.	Few assessment categories account for the relative factors of the learning experience.	Assessment categories do not account for all relevant factors of the learning experience.
Rubric Category Assessment Criteria	Assessment criteria for each category are clearly defined.	Assessment criteria for most of the categories (>50%) are clearly defined.	Assessment criteria for some of the categories (about 50%) are clearly defined.	Assessment criteria for few of the categories (<50%) are clearly defined.	Assessment criteria are not clearly defined for any category.
Rubric Category Importance/ Weight	The relative importance/ weight of each category is identified.	The relative importance/ weight of most categories (>50%) is identified.	The relative importance/ weight of some categories (about 50%) is identified.	The relative importance/ weight of few categories (<50%) is identified.	The relative importance/ weight is not identified for any category.
Rubric Performance Scale	Rubric scale clearly defines all levels of performance.	Rubric scale clearly defines most levels of performance.	Rubric scale clearly defines some levels of performance.	Rubric scale clearly defines few levels of performance.	Rubric scale does not clearly define levels of performance.
Rubric Scale Differentiation	Achievement at each level is clearly differentiated from that of the higher and lower levels.	Achievement at most levels is clearly differentiated from that of the higher and lower levels.	Achievement at few levels is clearly differentiated from that of the higher and lower levels.	Achievement at few levels is clearly differentiated from that of the higher and lower levels.	Achievement at each level is not clearly differentiated from that of higher and lower levels.
Rubric Scale Tone			Scale labels and details are positive.	Most scale labels and details are positive.	Scale labels and details are negative.

RUBRIC FOR GRADING PLAN
Developed with Elizabeth Seward and Edward Robinson

CATEGORY	3	2	1	0
Overall Quality of Grading Plan	Explanation of grading plan is clear and concise.	Explanation of grading plan is mostly clear.	Explanation of grading plan is vague.	Explanation of grading plan is not provided.
Description of Tests and Assignments	Description of tests and assignments is clear and concise.	Description of tests and assignments is mostly clear.	Description of tests and assignments is vague or incomplete.	Description of tests and assignments is not provided.
Explanation of Letter Grades	Explanation of points and percentages for grades is clear and concise.	Explanation of points and percentages for grades is mostly clear.	Explanation of points and percentages for grades is vague.	Explanation of points and percentages for grades is not provided.
Linking Graded Activities to Learning Objectives	All graded activities are linked to a learning objective.	Most graded activities are linked to a learning objective.	Some graded activities are linked to a learning objective.	No graded activities are linked to a learning objective.
Linking Learning Objectives to a Graded Activity	All learning objectives are linked to a graded activity.	Most learning objectives are linked to a graded activity.	Some learning objectives are linked to a graded activity.	No learning objectives are linked to a graded activity.
Mechanics	Grading plan is well written with no spelling or grammatical errors.	Grading plan has mostly well composed sentences with few spelling or grammatical errors.	Grading plan is poorly written with some spelling or grammatical errors.	Grading plan has many mistakes.

RUBRIC FOR BLUEPRINT FOR TESTS/OTHER EVALUATION
Developed with Kelly Thompson and Moana Vercoe

CATEGORY	4	3	2	1	0
Blueprint	Blueprint shows questions in correct cell of matrix.	Blueprint shows most questions in correct cell of matrix.	Blueprint shows some questions in correct cell of matrix.	Blueprint shows few questions in correct cell of matrix.	No blueprint or blueprint shows all questions inappropriately placed.
Question Appropriateness for Student Level	Blueprint displays questions that are appropriate for the level of students in course.	Almost all of the questions Blueprint displays are appropriate for the level of students in course.	Most of the questions Blueprint displays are appropriate for the level of students in course.	Only a few of the questions Blueprint displays are appropriate for the level of students in course.	Blueprint displays questions that are inappropriate for the level of students in course.
Content Validity— Test Coverage	Questions correspond to a representative sample of course material covered.	Questions correspond to a representative sample of 75% of material covered.	Questions correspond to a representative sample of 50–75% of material covered.	Questions concentrate on less than half of the material covered.	Questions include material not covered in class or included in course objectives.
Learning Objective Connection	Questions test the course learning objectives.	Almost all of the questions test the course learning objectives.	Most of the questions test the course learning objectives.	A few of the questions test the course learning objectives.	The questions do not test the course learning objectives.
Question Clarity	The questions are clear and easy to understand.	Almost all of the questions are clear and easy to understand.	Most of the questions are clear and easy to understand.	A few of the questions are clear and easy to understand.	The questions are not clear and easy to understand.

RUBRIC FOR CLASSROOM ASSESSMENT TECHNIQUES (CATs)

CATEGORY	5	3	1	0
Usefulness	Content, process, or ambience of class is directly assessed.	Content, process, or ambience of class is somewhat assessed.	Content, process, or ambience of class is barely assessed.	Content, process, or ambience of class is not assessed.
Tone	Question is phrased in constructive way.	Question is phrased in positive way.	Question is phrased in neutral way.	Question is phrased in negative way.
Instructions	Instructions are clear and concise.	Most of the instructions are clear.	Instructions are vague.	No instructions are given.
Learning Objective	CAT is linked to a learning objective.	CAT is somewhat linked to a learning objective.	CAT is barely linked to a learning objective.	CAT is not linked to a learning objective.
Appropriateness	CAT asks question students are able to answer.	CAT asks question most students are able to answer.	CAT asks question few students are able to answer.	CAT asks question no student can answer.

RUBRIC FOR TEACHING>< LEARNING PHILOSOPHY FOR COURSE
Developed with Paul Whitman, Robin Owens, Dorothea Viale, and Erin Andrade-Lopez

CATEGORY	3	2	1	0
Explains Instructor's Overall Concept of Learning	Instructor's overall concept of learning, including roles of student, teacher, and design of learning experiences, is explained in significant detail.	Most of these aspects are explained in moderate detail.	Some of these aspects are superficially explained.	These aspects of the concept of learning are not explained.
Students' Best Learning	Various learning styles or intelligences are provided on how students best represent information in their minds.	Most learning styles or intelligences are provided on how students best represent information in their minds.	Some learning styles or intelligences are provided on how students best represent information in their minds.	Few learning styles or intelligences are provided on how students best represent information in their minds.
Types of Learning in Field	Types of learning in the field are significantly described using multiple learning theories.	Types of learning in the field are moderately described with some theoretical support.	Types of learning in the field are superficially described with very little learning theory support.	Types of learning in the field are not described using learning theory.
Types of Learners in Field	Types of learners in the field are significantly described using multiple learning theories.	Types of learners in the field are moderately described with some theoretical support.	Types of learners in the field are superficially described with very little learning theory support.	Types of learners in the field are not described using learning theory.
Hopes and Dreams	The philosophy of teaching and learning explicitly addresses teaching goals and learning objectives.	The philosophy of teaching and learning addresses some teaching goals and learning objectives.	The philosophy of teaching and learning vaguely addresses teaching goals and learning objectives.	The philosophy of teaching and learning does not address teaching goals and learning objectives.
Clarity of Learning Objectives	What the student will be responsible for learning is precisely defined.	What the student will be responsible for learning is mostly defined.	What the student will be responsible for learning is vaguely defined.	What the student will be responsible for learning is not defined.
Implementations Make This Happen	An explicit plan on how the instructor will connect teaching with his or her philosophy of learning is provided.	Some plan on how the instructor will connect teaching with his or her philosophy of learning is provided.	A vague plan on how the instructor will connect teaching with his or her philosophy of learning is provided.	No plan on how the instructor will connect teaching with his or her philosophy of learning is provided.
Reasons for Choices	Explicit reasons for the choices made on how the instructor will connect teaching with his or her learning philosophy are provided.	Some reasons for the choices made on how the instructor will connect teaching with his or her learning philosophy are provided.	Vague reasons for the choices made on how the instructor will connect teaching with his or her learning philosophy are provided.	No reasons for the choices made on how the instructor will connect teaching with his or her learning philosophy are provided.
Professional Development Plans	What future instructional development and Scholarship of Teaching and Learning will be studied for effective teaching is clearly addressed.	What future instructional development and Scholarship of Teaching and Learning will be studied for effective teaching is addressed.	What future instructional development and Scholarship of Teaching and Learning will be studied for effective teaching is vaguely addressed.	What future instructional development and Scholarship of Teaching and Learning will be studied for effective teaching is not addressed.

References

Alexander, P. A., & Murphy, P. K. (1998). The research base for APA's Learner-Centered Psychological Principles. In N. Lamberts & B. L. McCombs (Eds.), *How students learn: Reforming schools through learner-centered education* (pp. 25–60). Washington, DC: American Psychological Association.

American Library Association (ALA). (2000). *Information literacy standards for higher education ACRL 2000* [Online]. Available: http://www.ala.org/acrl/ilcomstan.html.

Anderson, L. W., & Krathwohl, D. R. (Eds.). (2001). *A taxonomy for learning, teaching, and assessing: A revision of Bloom's Taxonomy of Educational Objectives.* New York: Addison Wesley Longman.

Anderson, R. S., & Speck, B. W. (Eds.). (1998, Summer). *Changing the way we grade student performance: Classroom assessment and the new learning paradigm.* New Directions for Teaching and Learning, No. 74. San Francisco: Jossey-Bass.

Andrews, J. D. W. (1980, Fall/Winter). The verbal structure of teacher questions: Its impact on class discussion. *POD Quarterly, 2*(3&4), 129–163.

Angelo, T. A., & Cross, K. P. (1993). *Classroom assessment techniques: A handbook for college teachers* (2nd ed.). San Francisco: Jossey-Bass.

Astin, A. W. (1977). *Four critical years.* San Francisco: Jossey-Bass.

Bain, K. (2004). *What the best teachers do.* Cambridge, MA: Harvard University Press.

Barkley, E., Clifton, A., deCourcy, A., & Kloos, M. (1998). A declaration of interdependence: Philosophy and practice of interdisciplinary team teaching. *Journal on Excellence in College Teaching, 9*(1), 87–103.

Barr, R. B., & Tagg, J. (1995). From teaching to learning: A new paradigm for undergraduate education. *Change, 27,* 6.

Bean, J. C., & Peterson, D. (1998, Summer). Grading classroom participation. In R. S. Anderson & B. W. Speck (Eds.), *Changing the way we grade student performance: Classroom assessment and the new learning par-*adigm (pp. 33–40). New Directions for Teaching and Learning, No. 74. San Francisco: Jossey-Bass.

Beidler, P. G. (1986, Winter). "As long as there is personal engagement": The way students learn. In P. G. Beidler (Ed.), *Distinguished teachers on effective teaching* (pp. 51–61). New Directions for Teaching and Learning, No. 28. San Francisco: Jossey-Bass.

Belenky, M. F., Clinchy, B. M., Goldberger, N. R., & Terule, J. M. (1986). *Women's ways of knowing.* New York: Basic Books.

Bender. T. (2003). *Discussion-based online teaching to enhance student learning: Theory, practice, and assessment.* Sterling, VA: Stylus.

Bligh, D. A. (2000). *What's the use of lectures?* San Francisco: Jossey-Bass.

Bloom, B. S., & Krathwohl, D. R. (1956). *Taxonomy of Educational Objectives: The classification of educational goals, by a committee of college and university examiners. Handbook I: Cognitive Domain.* New York: Longman Green.

Bonwell, C. C., & Eison, J. A. (1991). *Active learning: Creating excitement in the classroom.* ASHE-ERIC Higher Education Report No. 1. Washington, DC: The George Washington University, School of Education and Human Development.

Bowen, H. R. (1977). *Investment in learning.* San Francisco: Jossey-Bass.

Boyer, E. L. (1990). *Scholarship reconsidered: Priorities of the professoriate.* Princeton, NJ: Carnegie Foundation for the Advancement of Teaching.

Carson, B. H. (1999). Bad news in the service of good teaching: Students remember ineffective professors. *Journal on Excellence in College Teaching, 10*(1), 91–105.

Cashin, W. E. (1985). *Improving lectures.* Kansas State University Idea Paper No. 14. Manhattan, KS: Kansas State University Center for Faculty Evaluation and Development.

Cerbin, W. (1994). The course portfolio as a tool for continuous improvement in teaching and learning. *Journal on Excellence in College Teaching, 5*(1), 95–105.

Chapman, D. W. (2000). Designing problems for motivation and engagement in the PBL classroom. *Journal on Excellence in College Teaching, 11*(2&3), 73–82.

Chickering, A. W., & Gamson, Z. F. (1987). Seven principles for good practice in undergraduate education. *AAHE Bulletin, 39*(7), 3–7.

Chickering, A. W., & Gamson, Z. F. (1991, Fall). Institutional Inventory. In A. W. Chickering & Z. F. Gamson (Eds.), *Applying the Seven Principles for Good Practice in undergraduate education* (p. 87). New Directions in Teaching and Learning, No. 47. San Francisco: Jossey-Bass.

Chism, N. V. (1989, June). Large enrollment classes: Necessary evil or not necessarily evil? *Notes on Teaching* (pp. 1–7). Columbus, OH: Center for Teaching Excellence, Ohio State University (ERIC Document Reproduction Service No. ED 334 875).

Clinchy, B. M. (1990). Issues of gender in teaching and learning. *Journal on Excellence in College Teaching, 1,* 52–67.

Cockroft, W. H. (Ed.). (1982). *Mathematics counts.* London: Her Majesty's Stationery Office.

Cole, L. P. (1997). Heartland Community College Reading Program Curriculum Summary. Normal, IL: Heartland Community College. Available: http://www.hcc.cc.il.us/asc/reading_curriculum.pdf.

Combs, H. W., & Bourne, S. G. (1994). The renaissance of educational debate: Results of a five-year study of the use of debate in business education. *Journal on Excellence in College Teaching, 5*(1), 57–67.

Cornell, P. (2002, Winter). The impact of changes in teaching and learning on furniture and the learning environment. In N. V. Chism & D. J. Bickford (Eds.), *The importance of physical space in creating supportive learning environments* (pp. 33–42). New Directions for Teaching and Learning, No. 92. San Francisco: Jossey-Bass.

Costin, F. (1972, January). Lecturing versus other methods of teaching: A review of research. *British Journal of Educational Technology, 24,* 18–21.

Cottell, P. G., Jr. (1996). A union of collaborative learning and cooperative learning. *Journal on Excellence in College Teaching, 7*(1), 1–3.

Cox, M. D. (2004, Spring). Introduction to faculty learning communities. In M. D. Cox & L. Richlin (Eds.), *Building faculty learning communities* (pp. 5–23). New Directions for Teaching and Learning, No. 97. San Francisco: Jossey-Bass.

Dave, R. H. (1970). Psychomotor taxonomy. In R. J. Armstrong (Ed.), *Developing and writing behavioural objectives* (pp. 33–34). Tucson, AZ: Educational Innovators Press.

Diaz, D. P., & Cartnal, R. B. (n.d.). *Comparing student learning styles in an online distance learning class and an equivalent on-campus class* [On-line]. Available: http://www.collegedegreeguide.com/articles-fr/styles.htm.

Doolittle, P., & Chambers, M. (2004). Web-based instruction: Emphasizing pedagogy in a technological environment—A message from the guest editors. *Journal on Excellence in College Teaching, 15*(1), 1–6.

Eck, J. C. (2000). A sample of assessment findings related to Samford University's Problem-Based Learning Initiative. *PBL Insight: A Newsletter for Undergraduate Problem-Based Learning from Samford University, 3*(3), 12–13.

Ehninger, D., & Brochriede, W. (1972). *Decision by debate.* New York: Dodd, Mead.

Fabry, V. J., Eisenbach, R., Curry, R. R., & Golich, V. L. (1997). Thank you for asking: Classroom Assessment Techniques and students' perceptions of learning. *Journal on Excellence in College Teaching, 8*(1), 3–21.

Fink, L. D. (2003). *Creating significant learning experiences: An integrated approach to designing college courses.* San Francisco: Jossey-Bass.

Fisch, L. (1989, October). *Beth's midterm.* Paper presented at the annual meeting of the Professional and Organizational Development (POD) Network in Higher Education, Jekyll Island, GA.

Fiske, N.T., & Taylor, S. E. (1984). *Social cognition.* New York: Random House.

Gardner, H. (1993). *Frames of mind: The theory of multiple intelligences* (10th Anniversary ed.). New York: Basic Books.

Gardner, H. (2004). *Changing minds: The art and science of changing our own and other people's minds.* Boston: Harvard Business School Press.

Grasha, A. F. (1972). Observations on relating teaching goals to student response styles and classroom methods. *American Psychologists, 27,* 144–147.

Grasha, A. F. (1996). *Teaching with style: A practical guide to enhancing learning by understanding teaching and learning styles.* Claremont, CA: Alliance Publishers (www.iats.com).

Hacker, D. J., & Niederhauser, D. S. (2000, Winter). Promoting deep and durable learning in the online classroom. In R. E. Weiss, D. S. Knowlton, & B. W. Speck (Eds.), *Principles of effective teaching in the online classroom* (pp. 53–63). New Directions for Teaching and Learning, No. 84. San Francisco: Jossey-Bass.

Harrow, A. (1972). *A taxonomy of the psychomotor domain: A guide for developing behavioral objectives.* New York: McKay.

Jacobs, L. C., & Chase, C. I. (1992). *Developing and using tests effectively: A guide for faculty.* San Francisco: Jossey-Bass.

Johnson, D. W., Johnson, R., & Smith, K. (1991). *Cooper-*

ative learning: Increasing college faculty instructional activity. ASHE-ERIC Higher Education Report No. 4. Washington, DC: George Washington University, School of Education and Human Development.

Johnson, D. W., Johnson, R., & Smith, K. (1998). *Active learning: Cooperation in the college classroom.* Edina, MN: Interaction Book Company.

Kalina, M. L., & Catlin, A. (1994, May–June). The effects of the Cross-Angelo model of classroom assessment on student outcomes: A study. *Assessment Update, 6*(3), 21–24.

Kaminski, S. H. (2003). *PowerPoint presentations: The good, the bad and the ugly* [Online]. Available: http://www .shkaminski.com/Classes/Handouts/powerpoint.htm.

Kloss, R. J. (1994). A nudge is best: Helping students through the Perry Scheme of Intellectual Development. *College Teaching 42*(4), 151–158.

Knapper, C. K. (1995). The origins of teaching portfolios. *Journal on Excellence in College Teaching, 6*(1), 45–56.

Knisley, J. (2002). A four-stage model of mathematical learning. *The Mathematics Educator, 12*(1), 11–16. Athens, GA: Mathematics Education Student Association, The University of Georgia.

Kolb, D. A. (1984). *Experiential learning: Experience as the source of learning and development.* Englewood Cliffs, NJ: Prentice-Hall.

Krathwohl, D. R., Bloom, B. S., & Masia, B. B. (1964). *Taxonomy of educational objectives: The classification of educational goals. Handbook II: Affective domain.* New York: McKay.

Kuh, G. (1991). Teaching and learning—After class. *Journal on Excellence in College Teaching, 2*, 35–51.

Kurfiss, J. G. (1988). *Critical thinking: Theory, research, practice and possibilities.* ASHE-ERIC Higher Education Report No. 2, Washington, DC: American Association for the Study of Higher Education.

Lambiotte, J., & Dansereau, D. (1992). Effects of knowledge maps and prior knowledge on recall of science lecture content. *Journal of Experimental Education, 60*, 189–201.

Laughner, T. C. (2003). Learning spaces at the University of Notre Dame. In D. B. Brown (Ed.), *Developing faculty to use technology* (pp. 150–152). Bolton, MA: Anker.

Learnativity. (2002). http://www.learnativity.com/ learningstyles.html.

LeBlanc, P. (1988). How to get the words just right: A reappraisal of word process and revision. *Computers and Composition, 5*(3), 29–42.

Light, R. J., Wilett, J. B., & Singer, J. D. (1990). *By design: Planning research on higher education.* Cambridge, MA: Harvard University Press.

Litke, R. A. (1995). Learning lessons from students: What they like most and least about large classes. *Journal on Excellence in College Teaching, 6*(2), 113–129.

Lowman, J. (1994). Professors as performers and motivators. *College Teaching 42,* 137–141.

Lowman, J. (1995). *Mastering the techniques of teaching.* San Francisco: Jossey Bass.

Mathematics Council of the Alberta Teachers' Association. (1996). *Mathematical literacy . . . An idea to talk about* [Online]. Available: http://www.mathteachers.ab.ca/ MCATA%20referent%20paper.pdf.

Matlin, M. (1991). The social cognition approach to stereotypes and its application to teaching. *Journal on Excellence in College Teaching, 2*, 9–24.

McFann, J. (2005). *Revised Bloom Taxonomy.* Paper presented at the Southern California Professional Developers' Learning Community, Claremont, CA.

Millis, B. J. (1991). Fulfilling the promise of the "Seven Principles" through cooperative learning: An action agenda for the university classroom. *Journal on Excellence in College Teaching, 2*, 139–144.

Morrison, G. R., & Ross, S. M. (1998, Summer). Evaluating technology-based processes and products. In R. S. Anderson & B. W. Speck (Eds.), *Changing the way we grade student performance: Classroom assessment and the new learning paradigm* (pp. 69–77). New Directions for Teaching and Learning, No. 74. San Francisco: Jossey-Bass.

Murray-Harvey, R., & Slee, P. T. (2005). Introducing problem-based learning to teacher education: A case study. *Journal on Excellence in College Teaching, 16*(2), 33–54.

Organization for Economic Co-Operation and Development Program for International Student Assessment (OECD/PISA). (2003). *The PISA assessment framework—Mathematics, reading, science and problem solving knowledge and skills.* Paris: OECD.

Pace, R. C. (1979). *Measuring outcomes of college: Fifty years of findings and recommendations for the future.* San Francisco: Jossey-Bass.

Palloff, R. M., & Pratt, K. (1999). *Building communities in cyberspace: Effective strategies for the online classroom.* San Francisco: Jossey-Bass.

Perry, W. G., Jr. (1968/1970). *Forms of intellectual and ethical development in the college years: A scheme.* New York: Holt, Rinehart, and Winston.

Pollio, H. (1986, Fall). Practical poetry: Metaphoric thinking in science, art, literature, and nearly everywhere else. In *Teaching/Learning Issues, 60.* Knoxville, TN: The University of Tennessee Learning Research Center.

Quantitative Literacy Design Team. (2001). The case for quantitative literacy. In L. A. Steen (Ed.), *Mathematics and democracy: The case for quantitative literacy* (pp. 1–22). Princeton, NJ: The Woodrow Wilson National Fellowship Foundation, National Council on Education and the Disciplines, Mathematical Association of America.

Richlin, L. (1993, November). *The ongoing cycle of scholarly teaching and the scholarship of teaching.* Closing plenary presentation at the thirteenth annual Lilly Conference on College Teaching, Miami University, Oxford, OH.

Richlin, L. (1998). *Scholarly teaching and the "scholarship of teaching": Where Boyer gets muddled.* Paper presented at the national conference of the Professional and Organizational Development Network, Snowbird, UT.

Richlin, L. (2001, Summer). Scholarly teaching and the scholarship of teaching. In C. Kreber (Ed.), *Scholarship revisited: Perspectives on the scholarship of teaching* (pp. 57–68). New Directions for Teaching and Learning, No. 86. San Francisco, CA: Jossey-Bass.

Richlin, L., & Manning, B. (1995). *Improving a college/university teaching evaluation system: A comprehensive, developmental curriculum for faculty and administrators.* Claremont, CA: Alliance Publishers (www.iats.com).

Ronkowski, S. A. (1993). Scholarly teaching: Developmental stages of pedagogical scholarship. In L. Richlin (Ed.), *Preparing faculty for the new conceptions of scholarship* (pp. 79–90). New Directions for Teaching and Learning, No. 54. San Francisco: Jossey-Bass.

Salisbury-Glennon, J. D., Young, A. J., & Stefanou, C. R. (2001). Creating contexts for motivation and self-regulated learning in the college classroom. *Journal on Excellence in College Teaching, 12*(2), 19–35.

Schaible, R., & Robinson, B. D. (1995). Collaborating teachers as models for students. *Journal on Excellence in College Teaching, 6*(1), 9–16.

Schnoeder, H., & Ebert, D. G. (1983). Debates as a business and society teaching techniques. *Journal of Business Education, 58,* 266–269.

Simpson, E. J. (1972). *The classification of educational objectives in the psychomotor domain.* Washington, DC: Gryphon House.

Sorcinelli, M. D. (1991, Fall). Research findings on the seven principles. In A. W. Chickering & Z. F. Gamson (Eds.), *Applying the seven principles for good practice in undergraduate education* (pp. 13–25). New Directions in Teaching and Learning, No. 47. San Francisco: Jossey-Bass.

Speck, B. W. (2002). *Facilitating students' collaborative writing.* ASHE-ERIC Higher Education Report, *28*(6). San Francisco: Jossey-Bass.

STLHE. (1996). *Ethical principles in university teaching.* Vancouver: Society for Teaching and Learning in Higher Education.

Suskie, L. (2004). *Assessing student learning: A common sense guide.* Bolton, MA: Anker Publishing.

Svinicki, M. (2004). *Learning and motivation in the postsecondary classroom.* Bolton, MA: Anker.

Svinicki, M., Sullivan, T., Greer, M., & Diaz, M. (1991, November). *Combining departmental training with central support: A research project.* Paper presented at the Third National Conference on the Training and Employment of Graduate Teaching Assistants, Austin, TX.

Treagust, D. F., & Fraser, B. J. (1986, April). *Validation and application of the College and University Classroom Environment Inventory (CUCEI).* Paper presented at the 76th annual meeting of the American Educational Research Association, San Francisco.

Unruh, D. (1988). *Test scoring manual: Guide for developing and scoring course examinations.* Los Angeles: Office of Instructional Development, UCLA.

Walvoord, B. E. (2004). *Teaching well, saving time: Two powerful principles.* Keynote presentation at the national Lilly Conference on College Teaching at Miami University, Oxford, Ohio.

Walvoord, B. E., & Anderson, V. J. (1998). *Effective grading: A tool for learning and assessment.* San Francisco: Jossey-Bass.

Wulff, D. H., Nyquist, J. D., & Abbott, R. D. (1987). Students' perceptions of large classes. In M. G. Weimer (Ed.), *Teaching large classes well,* New Directions for Teaching and Learning, no. 32 (pp. 17–30). San Francisco: Jossey-Bass.

Zull, J. E. (2002). *The art of changing the brain: Enriching the practice of teaching by exploring the biology of learning.* Sterling, VA: Stylus.

ASSOCIATIONS

International Alliance of Teacher Scholars (IATS)
  http://www.iats.com
Professional and Organizational Development (POD)
Network in Higher Education
  http://www.podnetwork.org
Society for Teaching and Learning in Higher Education (STLHE)
  http://www.mcmaster.ca/stlhe/welcome.htm

Glossary of Course Design Terms

Active Learning. According to Bonwell and Eison (1991), "anything that involves students in doing things and thinking about the things they are doing" (p. 2). Fink (2003) separates active learning into experiences and reflection (p. 104).

Blueprint. Plan for building a structure to serve a particular purpose.

Blueprint for Learning. Plan for building a course to promote and document learning.

Classroom Assessment Techniques (CATs). Method developed by Angelo and Cross (1993) to provide real-time feedback to an instructor and students on how a course is going. Involves short, anonymous responses by students to questions posed by the instructor.

Critical Thinking. Careful judgment or judicious evaluation of information.

Developmental Taxonomies/Models. Steps or stages of increasing ability. These are Cognitive (intellectual development), Affective (psychological and ethical development), and Psychomotor (physical and process development).

Educational Paradigms. Described by Barr and Tagg (1995). There are two paradigms: Instructional Paradigm, which focuses on traditional teacher-centered education; and Learning Paradigm, which focuses on student learning outcomes.

Evaluation Plan (EP). Tests, assignments, and grading system used to assess how students reach the course learning objectives.

Experiential Learning. Learning by doing an authentic task.

Information Literacy. The ability to search for and evaluate the quality of information.

Interdisciplinary Teaching. Collaborative design and conduct of a course by two or more instructors from different disciplines.

Learning. A physical change in the brain. Demonstrated as a change of behavior.

Learning Communities. *Student* communities range from groups of students taking two or more courses together to groups of students who live together and complete a specified curriculum as a cohort. *Faculty* communities are yearlong groups of 8 to 12 faculty members and can be "cohorts" of faculty members at a particular stage of their career or "topic based," focusing on a specific teaching><learning concern or skill.

Learning Environment. Classroom, out-of-classroom, and online elements that affect students' ability to meet course learning objectives.

Learning Experiences (LEs). Activities designed to assist students in achieving the course learning objectives. These activities may be passive or active.

Learning Objectives (LOs). Specified abilities that students will achieve, phrased as "after completing this course, students will be able to . . .". They must be as observable and measureable as possible and criteria must be clearly described in a rubric.

Learning Styles. Preferred learning experiences.

Motivation. Intrinsic motivation emphasizes internal rewards. Behavior is performed based on personal goals and values. Extrinsic motivation is encouraged by an outside source. Behavior is performed based on the expectation of outside reward, such as money or grades.

Multiple Intelligences. Nine categories of human abilities, each of which can be destroyed or at a genius level without affecting the others: verbal-linguistic, mathematical-logical, musical, visual-spatial, bodily-kinesthetic, naturalistic, intrapersonal, interpersonal, and existential. Developed by Howard Gardner (1993, 2004).

Portfolios. *Student portfolios* include a variety of materials demonstrating how the student has met the course learning objectives. Course portfolios include information on the design and implementation of a specific course. *Teaching portfolios* include a selection of course portfolios with additional information such as the instructor's overall teaching philosophy and professional development plan.

Problem-Based Learning (PBL). "[A] focused, experientially-based learning organized around the presentation, investigation, and resolution of real-world problems" (Murray-Harvey & Slee, 2005).

Quantitative Literacy. Sometimes called numeracy or mathematical literacy. "[T]he capacities of students to analyze, reason, and communicate ideas effectively as they pose, formulate, solve, and interpret mathematical problems in a variety of situations" (OECD/PISA, 2003, p. 24).

Questions. *Convergent questions* have a "correct" answer (one agreed upon by experts). This type of question is not discussable. *Divergent questions* are ones whose answer is disagreed upon by experts, based on how they value the evidence. In a discussion, positions are proposed with reasoning and critical analysis.

Rubric. Sets out elements and criteria for an assignment.

Scholarly Cycle of Course (Re)design. Steps in building a course through scholarly teaching. If the results are worth sharing, it results in the Scholarship of Teaching and Learning (SoTL). Includes using results to redesign the course for better student learning.

Scholarly Teaching. Using a scholarly process to set goals and objectives, consult literature, choose learning experiences, document results, and use results to improve student learning in the course the next time it is taught.

Scholarship of Teaching and Learning (SoTL). Publication or presentation of results of scholarly teaching.

Teaching Goals (TGs). Developed from the big questions in the discipline and lead to student learning objectives. Do not need to be observable or measurable.

Teaching><Learning (T><L) Connection. The interplay between aspects of an instructor's teaching activities and the learning needs of students.

Teaching Metaphor. An analogy for the teaching><learning connection.

Teaching Style. Instructor's preferred types of learning experiences to use in course.

Team Teaching. Collaborative design and conduct of a course by two or more instructors from the same or different disciplines.

Transdisciplinarity. Pushing multiple perspectives beyond disciplinary thinking, particularly to focus on otherwise insoluble socially significant problems.

Variables. *Subject variables* are the actual characteristics of individual people, such as age, political view, work experience, and learning style. *Stimulus variables* are the perception of the onlooker and come from family attitudes, experience with people different from ourselves, and education.

Index